W9-CJP-348

Becoming a Father

The Real Work of a Man's Soul

JOHN L. HART, Ph.D.

Health Communications, Inc.
Deerfield Beach, Florida

www.hci-online.com

"With Kit, Age 7, at the Beach" ©1970, 1998 by the Estate of William
  Stafford. Reprinted from *The Way It Is: New and Selected Poems* by
  William Stafford with the permission of Graywolf Press, Saint Paul,
  Minnesota.

LI-YOUNG LEE: "The Gift" ©1986 by Li-Young Lee. Reprinted from
  ROSE, with permission of BOA Editions, Ltd., 260 East Ave.,
  Rochester, NY 14604.

Library of Congress Cataloging-in-Publication Data

Hart, John L., date.
  Becoming a father : the real work of a man's soul / John L. Hart.
      p.   cm.
  Includes bibliographical references.
  ISBN 1-55874-619-6 (tradepaper)
  1. Fatherhood—Religious aspects—Christianity.   2. Joseph, Saint.
I. Title.
BV4529.17H37   1998
248.8'421—DC21   98–41238
                                                                CIP

©1998 John L. Hart
ISBN 1-55874-619-6

Publisher: Health Communications, Inc.
            3201 S.W. 15th Street
            Deerfield Beach, FL 33442-8190

Cover design by Lawna Oldfield

Contents

Acknowledgments

I would like to thank the many people who have helped to shape *Becoming a Father.*

This book is the sum of many parts. It goes back at least as far as my two grandfathers. The Reverend Hamilton was an Iowa horseback Methodist minister, who baptized people in rivers, wrote poetry, and loved the study of psychology and dreams. Orlie Hart was a deacon in his church, a black-smith, a farmer and a great storyteller, and a grandfather who took lots of time to show his grandson the wonders of Oregon nature. Coach Pete Janin was a man who opened his home to lonely Little League ballplayers. Coaches Paul Poetsch and Coach Roy Helser spent countless hours after school and during the summers with boys who needed their guidance and skills in becoming young men with pride and self-esteem.

We find many fathers and friends along the way. Robert Bly encouraged my poetry, my writing and my work. Mel Henry provided encouragement and friendship. Charlie Bensley, Gunnar Cramer, Dag Furuholmen, Bill Mairs, Steve Smith and Bruce Schmidt are the best of friends and helped more than they know with this book. I especially thank Berger Hareide for his guidance, spiritual strength, knowledge of

Christian literature, inspiration and steadfast friendship. Thank you Joseph Hart for everything.

Thank you Shirley Bell, Jill Penkus, Nancy Hart and Connie Nicholas Carnes for guidance, inspiration and heartfelt support.

I thank Sharron Barefoot for her many hours of typing.

I would like to thank Lakshmi Narayan, Head Librarian of the Krotona Library in Ojai, California, for her thoughtful guidance and assistance in finding research materials.

Jack Canfield deserves special thanks for his support and encouragement with this project. I would like to thank Peter Vegso of Health Communications for believing in this project.

Thank you Matthew Diener for your special vision, your encouragement, insights and guidance as my editor.

And a very special thank you to Andrea Torokvei for: her love, becoming my wife, helping me create this book, always being there for me, and helping me to believe. Special thanks as well to Nick Torokvei for letting me be one of the men in your life.

And I thank God every day for my beautiful daughter Kelly Lara Hart for all the joy, laughter and love she has given me, and the fatherhood you have brought me.

Introduction

Dear Reader: The Books of Joseph are fiction. I wrote them with respect and admiration for the biblical figure of Joseph. They are the products of my imagination. I wrote them after reading and prayer on Sunday mornings and they became an important spiritual exercise for me. I sincerely hope that no one is offended by my interpretation of this ancient and sacred story, for none is intended. I want only to show how important fathers are to the raising of their children. I have taken poetic and imaginative jumps, and this story of Joseph is neither theologically nor historically perfect.

I am a father, a poet, college professor and Vietnam veteran. I tried to write a story that contemporary fathers could hear and appreciate. We need fathers all of our lives and there are so many children who need one right now. I hope in the story of Joseph and Jesus you can hear yourself and your child.

The Stages of Fatherhood

1. Acknowledgment or Denial
2. Role Acceptance (Providing and Protecting) or Rejection
3. Bonding and Connectedness and Boundaries
4. Emotional Coaching of the Personal, Moral and Spiritual Intelligences
5. Fatherhood and Mentoring

The stages of fatherhood are not to be seen as steps carved in stone. Like all developmental stages the levels are really passages that should be seen more like a spiral than steps. As a man passes from one stage to the next it is certainly entirely possible to go backwards or to jump ahead two or more stages. Someone might even be in two different stages simultaneously.

For example, a man might completely be in Stage One— denial of paternity of one child he has fathered with one woman—and then and at the same time be at Stage Two in acceptance of the role of father for another child with another woman. A man can even be in different stages of development with different children within his family. Certainly many daughters and some sons in our paternalistic society find themselves with fathers who reject them while bonding and connecting with their sibling.

I believe, however, that the stages give us a working guide

to different levels of fathering on an emotional, behavioral, moral and spiritual level. We should consider the interactive dynamic of fathering. That means that fathering affects you as much as it does the child. A father who is in denial of being the father of a child he knows to be his own is carrying a bastard inside himself. His is not someone who could ever claim to be a man worthy of fatherhood. For the story of Joseph will show clearly that being a father develops the man as much as the father develops the child. A man in denial will carry a dark hole inside himself. A man rejecting will push away something inside his own self that needs to be acknowledged and to grow. A man that does not bond and connect will not develop his own personal, moral and spiritual intelligence. His heart and soul will be diminished.

Stage Five of fatherhood is a developmental level that encompasses the soul as well as the heart. This man watches out for all children in our society. It is a man who desires to raise well the next generation in his business, his profession, his craft or labor. It is a man who lives out the life of being the good father. It is a level of fathering to be reached for by each of us and by every society. We can thank Joseph, the earthly father of Jesus, for setting us a standard to strive towards.

PART I

FATHERHOOD AND ITS ROLES

1

The Child
Is Father of the Man

The child is father of the man.[1]

William Wordsworth

I n many ways, the first modern father was perhaps the most overlooked parent in history. He raised a child that was not his. He provided a home and raised him as if he were his own. He provided shelter of the old-fashioned kind because his stepson was from birth a fugitive and Joseph was there for him. He provided protection; he did anything and everything that was necessary.

He played with him. He helped him know what it meant to be a man and a decent human being. He raised him to be someone special, taught him his trade, took him fishing and didn't get in the way of his stepson's own destiny. Presumably, Joseph stood by, holding back his fatherly

---

1. William Wordsworth, "My Heart Leaps Up," in Angela Partington, ed., *The Oxford Dictionary of Quotations* (New York: Oxford University Press, 1992), 745.

instincts to fight and battle to save the life of this young man he must have dearly loved.

He stood by to hear the agony of the nails being driven in, and stood by during Jesus' suffering, spearing, and his slow dying. He was there hearing his stepson cry, "Father, why hast thou forsaken me?" Standing there, crying himself by now, and thinking does he mean me, does he want me to try to do something? Standing there, just standing there. For his own soul and his own destiny, he was standing there. Surely, this was the soul work of being Jesus' earthly father. A man named Joseph fulfilling his own life's work of being as good a father as he possibly could.

Your own work as a father will entail suffering and sacrifice and at some point standing by and watching your own child go their own way toward their own destiny. This will build your soul. I believe it is your fathering that will enable you to fulfill and complete yourself as a man.

It is sacred work. It is the real work of being a man.

It is too bad that Joseph's life with his stepson Jesus is not more known. The loving, the laughter, dinner times, and bath times when he was a baby and a little boy; showing the little boy how to hold a hammer and how to fish; helping him with what he knew about living. Picking the little boy up from hurts and disappointment and helping him deal with worries and bullies. All of this is soul work for a man. This book is about what that work is and some thoughts about how to do that work.

A Bunch of Joes

Unfortunately, I believe that fathers from the 1960s through the decades to today somehow inherited the other message about Joseph. We are superfluous. We are unimportant to the story of childrearing, we don't really matter in parenting, we are out of the picture. Mary is in all the paintings, in all the statues. Joseph just drove the donkey and arranged bad lodging at the inn. It is one of the tragedies of our times that fathers are not considered important to raising our children.

Contemporary fathers, whether biological parent or stepfather, have somehow come to be known as the least important parent. How did this come to be? We will talk more of this later in the book, but first let us consider what if we had the chance to sit down and listen to Joseph, if he could tell us his story.

Prologue:
Global Press International
Cairo, Egypt (For Immediate Release)

Mining Team Finds Buried Tomb

The National Museum of Egypt is reporting a mysterious and potentially extraordinary find. An oil research expedition near Alexandria reported that during blasting operations their seismic devices had revealed what appeared to be a buried tomb. A National Museum archaeologist accompanying the exploration temporarily halted any further blasting. The area was kept secured and untouched until the arrival of the Museums' Historical Site Exploration Team.

Secured and Intact with Seals Unbroken

After nearly two days of digging, what was unearthed was "a beautifully carved tomb with seals unbroken." Inside the tomb was a sarcophagus containing the body of a very old man who was dressed very simply and did not appear to be a noble or of any royal family in spite of the elaborate richness of the tomb. The senior archaeologist has come forward with little other information. Other unconfirmed sources report that the sarcophagus contained leather-bound primitive books called codices of potentially momentous historical importance. Journalists and media from all over the world are flocking to the site. There is said to be extremely tight security. All archaeologists and the original miners and workers on the site are sequestered.

Momentous Finding

One of the original archaeologists who asked to be anonymous said, "There are as many as four codices that were found in an exquisite wooden box in the sarcophagus with the body." The books are assumed to have been written by the entombed man. One official, asking not to be identified, said it sounds incredulous but the body is identified on the tomb inscription and on the sarcophagus as Joseph, father of Jesus of Nazareth.

The First Book of Joseph

[Translator's note: The words are carefully written in Greek and some Aramaic. They are written in a Roman style book called a codice that is separated into parts called tractates. The writing is personal, more like a diary or journal rather than scholarly.]

The light fades

the shadows deepen, and my hands are tired.

The scent of jasmine in the garden.

I have lit the old silver lamp, but my eyes can barely see to write.

I have just a little more to say

and then my part in this story without end is done.

I write this now, as a beginning to my books, long after I had finished them. I am an old man and soon to die. I will write no more. I have been blessed in this life with love, family and friendship. I believe these were God's gifts for caring for the child, Jesus. My books here were written at the request of the man known now as Jesus of Nazareth. He wanted me to tell my story, of my work of being his earthly father.

I will lay these books now in this cedar chest. It was a gift he made for me so many years ago. When I touch it, I remember the first time, his hands so small when we made things. . . . but that is in my story.

[Translator's note: THE FIRST TRACTATE OF THE FIRST CODICE. These pages are clearly older than the above and appear more clumsily written.]

My Story of Becoming a Father

It is strange for me with these scarred and broken hands of a carpenter to write. I am clumsy with pen and with the words, and the paper seems soft. It does not seem like something that can endure like wood. My son asked me to write this and so did my patron Kahlil and so I do this for them. Kahlil has helped me with the writing, but the words are mine and this is my story of being a father.

I have been guided and blessed by great dreams sent to me by God during my lifetime. It is the holy dreams that guided my life and my destiny. Mary and I had the raising of the child who was God's son and my earthly son, Jesus.

Mary

I was betrothed to Mary who was my beloved since we were children growing up together in our village. Even as a child, Mary was different from the others. She was independent, strong and always curious. She wanted to know everything and learn. It was difficult for her, for though she was always most feminine and lovely, there was also the desire there for knowledge. She might have been a rabbi if not born a woman. Any caravan that passed she would find a way to talk to the traders, to learn the new songs, new poems and the stories of far-away places. She somehow learned counting and arithmetic. She knew how to make letters and words and so she was always in trouble with those who wanted her only to be a poor simple woman. That she grew lovely only brought her more attention. Others wanted her, but she wanted only me.

My mother and father had died when I was a small boy. They had drowned in a sudden storm on the sea and my uncle had raised me. Mary had been my friend and my consolation in my sorrow. She would find me sitting by myself and would just sit by me. It was then that I think that my love for her started. We would walk when we were older up to the place high on the hill under the fragrant trees, look out over the sea and wait for the stars.

Perhaps my story really begins there. It was a day in spring, just a month before our wedding, when we met there to watch the sunset and see the new moon. It was there that she stood before me and told me she was with child.

Up until that moment, I had been only a youth, skilled with my hands and full of myself. Full of my skills with wood, full of my luck and pride in having Mary, full of the delight I secretly took in others' envy of my skill, my strength and the loveliness of my bride-to-be. It was as though I lived life seeing myself through the eyes of others, those who told me how special I was. I lived looking to see how others saw me.

When she said, "I am with child," my life turned. With those four words, my life, as I had planned it, was destroyed. I stood looking at her. Her face was radiant and she tried to say something else to me. I turned away looking out over the waters. I saw a bird plummeting into the water to take a fish. The water splashed up and sparkled in the setting sun.

Darkness

I cannot write that I am proud of how I acted then. I acted like any youth that believes life is only about himself. At first, I was unbelieving, then astonished, and then in a rage of jealousy and shame to have been cuckolded on the very eve of my marriage. The very way she told me infuriated me. How could she stand there? She should have come crawling on her knees. I shouted at her, I screamed every vile word for whore, harlot and bitch. I was spitting into her face that I hated her. I wanted her to suffer.

We stood together, I remember now, in a place of holy beauty. The sun was reddening the sky and light was shining through the clouds in a way that the earth and all the air around were glowing. It was as though light flowed from out of the sky and the sea and Mary herself, and yet I hated the light from her face. I despised her beauty and the fragility in the tears in her eyes as she asked for understanding.

I had no understanding. I struck her down and left her on her knees reaching out to me. There was no understanding in me, only rage and pain. It shames me now and brings tears to my eyes to write this and remember my dear Mary on her knees with her blood running down her face with her tears. I turned and left her there.

I went down the hill, my own tears on my face and my heart bleeding. I felt like killing. I wanted to go into our village, to drink wine at the inn with my friends, shout, curse and break things. I wanted to destroy her. In my righteousness, I could shame and destroy her and the little bastard she was carrying. I could gather my friends, we could go to the rabbi and then denounce her. We could stone her and the bastard she carried. She was unclean, dirty, the mother of a muzarim, *the excrement of the community. My righteous uncle would say that she deserved to die. Every stone I imagined shattering her like she had my life. It was my right. I had my honor to uphold and that of my family.*

When she was stoned and dead and the dogs, rats and birds had had their way, nothing would remain of her and the muzarim *and then I would be seen as wounded and yet righteous. It was not I who had fallen.*

I picked up stones as I stumbled down. I was hurling stones and screaming curses. As they shattered on the boulders I imagined it was Mary and saw her falling down and dying. I do not know why I did not turn toward the inn to find pity. Instead, I went into my own home, and taking my bedroll and water-skin, I walked out into the darkness toward the mountains.

2

Becoming a Father: The Stages of Fatherhood

*True fatherhood is evoked not by a
flexing of muscle, but by initiation into
family and culture in a profound
transformational way.*[1]

Thomas Moore

J oseph's is a story for all fathers. His lessons
are our lessons. The soul road he follows in
learning to be a good man, a good husband
and a good father is a way that all men travel to
develop their souls.

We can stand back, look at the story and simply read what he said. We can go closer, and read
the words and relate to Joseph and to the story.
We can also go deeper and then become the story.
All of us are Joseph.

If we take parts of Joseph's story and look
closer and deeper, perhaps we can hear more of
what he is saying to all of us.

---

1. Thomas Moore, *Care of the Soul* (New York: HarperCollins Publishers, 1992), 35.

17

Faith, belief, spirit and soul are parts of our lives that cannot be seen or measured and are seldom talked about.
Sometimes they are topics of church services and sometimes
prayers. Yet too often they are not even a part of our everyday
world. Only when a baby is born, someone we love dies, a terrible accident occurs or perhaps just misses us do we become
aware. We become aware that we always live in God's world.
We do not choose when we live in God's world, we live in it
at all times. We just repeatedly forget, until life or death or fate
or destiny suddenly shows us. Most of the time, though, we
live in a world that we believe we created. In contemporary
daily life, we live in a world of just ME. The Me World is the
World of One. It is the world of logical thought and ration-
ality and technology. It is the concrete world, the singular
world. This is the world of measurement and exactness and
planning and building. It is practical and serious and without
humor or spirit. It is the mechanical world of Newtonian
physics: the cosmos as machine and the body as machine.
There is no soul and no spirit.

This is the world of contemporary fathers: the workday
world of contemporary man. It is getting to work at eight
sharp, being at the meeting at exactly 10 A.M. and making a
plan, and drawing a chart and measuring ourselves against
the bottom line. This is a world of exactness and you can
count on it. There are expectations and values you can
depend upon. The World of One is the world of keeping
score. It is the world of knowing where you stand. It is a
world that every man knows and knows well. We have been
keeping score since we were little boys and it never ends.

Walking up the steep steps to a meeting recently, a

distinguished professor, well known in his field, stopped and sighed deeply and said only half jokingly, "I have to get up, get up these stairs and get it up everyday in every way. I guess being a man is having to prove it again everyday."

In the World of One, every man knows his score. There are all kinds of measurements and every man carries those around in his head feeling good or bad about himself depending on his score.

Joseph lived in a different time and a different place than now. He lived in a time where every day there was a sense of prayer, of death and suffering. He lived in a time where fate and the mystery of God were an everyday awareness. Nevertheless, he also lived in a world of men and in a world where men kept score. He, too, lived part of the time in the World of One.

Joseph begins his story of becoming a father feeling very good about his score in the World of One. He is going to marry his childhood sweetheart. He is young and strong and has good work. He has good skills and good prospects. He has big expectations and he has big plans for his life. Life could not look better from the mountaintop. Remember he says, "Perhaps my story really begins there." It is there on the mountaintop when Mary says, "I am with child," that Joseph's initiation into becoming a father begins.

The Stages of Fatherhood

1. Acknowledgment or Denial
2. Role Acceptance (Providing and Protecting) or Rejection
3. Bonding and Connectedness and Boundaries

4. Emotional Coaching of the Personal, Moral and Spiritual Intelligences

5. Fatherhood and Mentoring

Joseph begins his initiation into fatherhood at Stage One and at the level of denial. When he hears that Mary is pregnant everything in his world changes. Joseph says, "With those four words, 'I am with child,' my life as I had planned it was destroyed." The initiation begins and he cannot even acknowledge it. Joseph is suddenly and without warning thrust out of his comfortable World of One expectations into the World of Two, which is the world of relationship, and simultaneously into the World of Three, the world of soul and fate.

Jerusalem

She looked and saw Joseph the Carpenter in Nazareth and Mary
His espoused Wife. And Mary said, If thou put me away from thee
Dost thou not murder me? Joseph spoke in anger and fury. Should I
Marry a Harlot and an Adulteress? Mary answered, Art thou more
* pure*
Than thy Maker who forgiveth Sins and calls again Her that is Lost
Tho She hates. he calls her again in love. I love my dear Joseph
But he driveth me away from his presence. yet I hear the voice of
* God*
In the voice of my Husband. tho he is angry for a moment, he will not
Utterly cast me away. if I were pure, never could I taste the sweets
Of the Forgiveness of Sins! if I were holy! I never could behold the
* tears*
Of love! of him who loves me in the midst of his anger in the furnace
* of fire.[2]*

                                                    WILLIAM BLAKE

2. E. J. Ellis, *The Poetic Works of William Blake* (London: Chatto and Windus, 1906), 2: 372–374.

The World of Two, the world of relationship, is one where, as we all know, life is not always under our control. It is the nature of relationship. The World of Two is the world of feelings and emotions and psychology, the relationship of the inner to the outer, of sight and insight, and reflection and action. It is a world full of turmoil and contradictions. Joseph is suddenly immersed into this world in which there are two views of everything. There are two opinions, two sets of feelings, two sets of values, two senses of humor, two views of where to put the furniture and what kind of car to buy. It is a simple truth: The World of Two creates tension and conflict. Attraction and sexuality create tension. Relationship creates tension. However, it is a truth that men and women who are in love and entering relationship do not fully realize. It is a realization that takes a lifetime together to fully know. Joseph has not lived a lifetime. He is just beginning.

> *Marriage is not a love affair,*
> *It's an ordeal*
> *It is a religious exercise, a sacrament,*
> *the grace of participating in another life.*[3]

Joseph is not ready for marriage to Mary. He is not ready to be a father. He is in denial of his own fate and destiny. He wants the life he had imagined, not the one God has chosen for him. As he writes in the passage about Darkness, in retrospect he is not proud about the way he acts. He blames her and he wants her to suffer. He is in denial and he cannot see her or the light around them. He is in darkness.

3. Diane K. Osborn, ed., *A Joseph Campbell Companion: Reflections on the Art of Living* (New York: HarperCollins Publishers, 1991), 46–47.

Fatherlessness

Many of us are not ready to be fathers when a child comes. Many men do not even know their children need them to be fathers. Parenting projects of all types typically ignore or minimize the support of fathering in the family. While hospitals and community clinics routinely offer young women opportunities for education in mothering skills and emotionally support mothers in learning the role of being mothers, fathers are just as routinely ignored. This is as true in Norway and most of Europe as in the United States. The message to young men becoming fathers is that they really are not expected to be much of a parent, or even have much to do with the nurturing and care of their children. Parenting and the entire role and responsibility of child rearing has been ascribed to mothers. Indeed many men as well as many societies see the male role as primarily being one of economically supporting the family.

This may not have been as consequential in a time when most fathers worked on the family farm or when divorce was rare. Today, however, is a different time. A United States survey indicates that one of five fathers had not seen their children in more than a year. A survey of adolescents found that 52 percent of them had not seen their father in more than a year and that only 16 percent saw their father as often as once a week.

Believing themselves to be superfluous to the parenting and child-rearing task, many men of broken marriages leave behind not only their marriage but also their children. They walk out of their children's lives physically and emotionally. "The immensity of the problem can be captured in a single statistic: in just three decades, between 1960 and 1990, the percentage of children living apart from their biological fathers more than doubled, from 17 percent to 36 percent. By the turn of the century, nearly 50 percent of children may be going to sleep each evening without being able to say good night to their dads."[4] Sociologist David Popenoe says, "The decline of fatherhood is one of the most basic, unexpected and extraordinary social trends of our time. . . ."[5] He cites an array of studies that illustrate the devastating effects of fatherlessness on children and society.

Denial of fathering as an individual and as a society has enormous consequences on our children. Acknowledging that fathering is necessary and real is an important message in Joseph's story. God has sent a child who needs a father. At first, Joseph cannot accept that reality and he runs away. There are many runaway Josephs in our society today. Just to acknowledge the pregnancy, the mother and the child is a necessary first step to fatherhood and Joseph cannot. A question to ask yourself when you learn of the pregnancy of the woman you are involved with is this: Can I step up and acknowledge this woman, this pregnancy, this child? Can I accept this reality? Can I take the steps required on this road of the soul to become a father?

Let us return to Joseph's story and seek his answers to becoming a father.

---

4. David Popenoe, "A World Without Fathers," *Wilson Quarterly* 20.2 (Spring 1996): 12.
5. Popenoe, 12.

The Dark Road

I remember little about the night except that my mind was a pot of scorpions. Every thought I had of Mary was stinging and burning like fire. I was full of poison, rage and a grinding pity for myself. I walked until dawn. Two times I turned back determined to act upon my anger, eager to see Mary stoned, and then turning again, I went on.

The sun rising brought heat, but no light to me. I walked on, my mood dark, and I paid no attention to what I was doing or where I was. I overtook a small group of men. If I had been alert, I would have noticed them and what kind of men they were and simply avoided them. Instead, I walked right in on them and they immediately demanded what little I had. The largest of them, a broken-nosed pocked man grabbed for my pack. If there is one thing a carpenter has it is strong hands and arms and I twisted his arm in a certain way snapping the bone. Now the rest jumped on and snarling and screaming in my rage I broke another bone and a nose or two before being beat. I was left barely alive and naked. They knew the sun would torment me more than they could before I died.

The Burning Light

Wa Iaomer Elohim Iehi-Aor, Wa-Iehi-Aor.[6,7]

All day I lay in the sun
The light burned through me.
My broken bones ground together in my legs as I tried to crawl.
The torment of sun and thirst sucked my life from me.
Unbearable torment! I raved and sobbed dry tears.
My tongue swelled and filled my mouth like a dried fish.
With a knife, I would have cut my own arm just to drink the blood.
My life was leaving me and I welcomed it because I could not bear this agony.
My own blind rage had brought me to this death.
I prayed for God to take me.
The light burned through me.
I felt water on my swollen tongue and cracked lips. It flowed over my face and down my neck and over my chest, water and more water.

A caravan on its way to Alexandria; the camels and their drivers simply stepping over me as just another dead animal. There was no reason to stop and help me, no more than for a dying rat.

The man who stopped was no ordinary man. My first memories of him are of his light brown eyes and the taste of cool water. His name was Kahlil. He was among the wealthiest men in

---

6. Neil Douglas-Klotz, *Desert Wisdom: Sacred Middle Eastern Writings from the Goddess Through the Sufis* (New York: HarperCollins Publishers, 1995), 40.
7. [Translator's note: From Genesis ancient Hebrew, "And God said, Let there be light: and there was light."]

Alexandria. A physician, a merchant, and traveler and teacher, he was many things. He was a man of spirit and compassion. He brought me along with him to Alexandria; along the way he set my bones, healed my wounds and heard my pitiful story. Concerning Mary I remember he said only once "I hear that you love her."

I had said nothing of the sort; however, his words stayed with me.

As we neared Alexandria he said, "I would like to build a small house in my garden; perhaps you would teach me how. I will pay." I could not even speak to answer.

The Healing

In Alexandria, we worked together on this house in which I now am writing. We worked side by side—Kahlil, the master, and me, the carpenter. He carried every timber, broke his thumb and his nails. He learned the beauty of wood. He learned of grain, and the scent of cedar fresh cut. We had the finest of tools and the finest of materials. In the work I remembered myself and healed something broken within. I remembered how my own father and then my uncle taught me the hammer, and the saw and chisel and adz and the shaping and curving and carving of wood: the making of windows and doors and shelves. When we worked, we talked. Often we talked of things I had built—like beams, doors and windows. Sometimes, we talked of Mary and what had happened between us. Each time the wound seemed less sore and increasingly I would remember her sweetness, and the friendship we had shared all our lives. I missed her.

Kahlil was like an older brother. He was a wise and good man. He treated me as an equal and he became my friend. No man can grow without a friend. A good friend is like the other part of a marriage. A good friend knows the truth about you and tells you. He knows the sorrow and the aloneness of being a man and stands by that in you. Men sometimes are ashamed that they love one another, yet if you do not carry another man in your heart, you are weakened in life.

On the last evening of the building of the house, we mounted the carved cedar door. We sat outside in the garden drinking Egyptian beer to celebrate. As the sun was setting a strange star rose in the sky. The light from this was unlike anything I had ever seen. I remember we looked at one another knowing something but not what.

The First Dream

That night I dreamed the first great dream.

It was full of blinding light and blazing color like the star in the sky.

I was covered with bloody scorpions and my skin was burning in the sun.

My hands were filled with stones and I was consumed with killing thirst.

Then there was Mary and just behind her stood an angel.

*In the clear light, I could see Mary's face and her eyes and
how she loved only me.*

I felt in my heart how I loved her,

I dropped the stones.

The scorpions fell from my scorched body.

I walked toward her as if into a cool stream.

I dropped to my knees in front of her.

The Angel and Mary poured water over my head and burning body.

The pure sweet water filled every part of me.

The Angel said God is sending you and Mary a child

and like all children this child needs a man to be his father

*and he needs love and caring to bring him to manhood to ful-
fill his destiny.*

From my knees, I embraced Mary and the child within her.

I awoke shaking in the warm Egyptian night.

*I saw the new bright star and lay trembling with tears running
from my eyes.*

*I sat in the garden through the night with the fragrance of
jasmine,*

the light from the strange star all around me.

Home Coming

The morning the ship was to leave Alexandria was bright and clear.

The sun was cool in the autumn sky.

I was leaving Alexandria on one of Kahlil's ships.

I was sorry and sad to say goodbye to this man, who had

saved my life, restored my spirit and become my friend.

I looked in those wise eyes and I thought I would never see him again. "Travel well and safely, Joseph," he said as he embraced me. "I, too, saw the star and it means something for both of us."

I did not really think so. I was going back to marry Mary and to be a simple carpenter. I thought I had my life under control and on a path I knew again. I know now, though, that the way to get God to laugh is to tell him your plans for your life.

I sat on the bow bound for Galilee. Around me ships and boats set sail across the blue waters leaving lines of white waves in every direction. Each one seemed a line of destiny. Ahead of me were Mary and a life I could not have ever imagined.

[Translator's note: End of first tractate.]

Codice I Tractate II: Return to Galilee

And so I returned to Galilee.

It was late autumn.

Sky clear and bright deep blue.

The air was chill and the wind brisk.

Stepping off the ship, finally home, the voices, the language of my own people, the shouts and smells of spices and meats of the market—I was finally home.

All of life was ahead of me.

Although I wanted nothing but home and Mary, I stayed through that day working with the crew unloading the ship. I had saved the money from building the garden house, I did not know what the next months with a wife and baby would bring, and any money would only help. It turned out it was good that I worked there that day.

There is always gossip on the docks. Here the news from the world comes first, and though certainly mostly lies and stories, there is always the seed of truth. As I unloaded the goods from Alexandria, I talked with one of the dock men—as it turns out a cousin. "Your uncle," he said, "he has made life difficult for Mary and her family. He blames them for your leaving and has told everyone that you were shamed into leaving, that she is having a bastard from a caravanman." Here he slyly turned toward me and said, "And is it true?" The look on his face I did not much like but the look he saw on mine he liked even less and quickly turned away saying, "I only repeat what I hear from your uncle. He says everywhere that she is a harlot and the child a muzarim." At that my body burned. I broke his nose and then walked back onto the ship.

I thought, I am ashamed, I thought of going back to Egypt. What I had to face and to deal with here would be too much for me. A life of sly glances and smiles and whispers was not for me. What had Mary done to us? How was I to live with my uncle?

As my temper cooled, I again thought of Mary and my dream. Back to Egypt now was not the way of forgiveness, simply the way of a sheep. I love Mary, I thought, I can be the father of this child, I just have to have the courage.

I walked back to the dock to my cousin Isaac. "Isaac," I said,

"I did not leave Mary because I was ashamed of her. I left because I was ashamed for myself. The child is mine, I am the father, God gave us this child and I come back to be married and raise this child and care for Mary and the baby."

I had said it.

"The child is mine." I had said it again.

I turned my back and worked. The sweat was running from my body and I could hear the whispers behind my back. I left as the sun set. I am sure that the news that I was back and had claimed Mary and the child as my own would be home to my uncle's house before I could.

At my uncle's house there was a storm waiting for me. My uncle was a good man and had been a father to me since the death of his younger brother, my father. They had business together as carpenters. My mother and father had died in a storm while fishing. My uncle had taken me into his home and cared for me as one of his own and taught me to be a carpenter. As I say, he was a good man, but in that way that some men are of being too good. In that I mean there were the rules of right and wrong and he knew the way of right and was righteous always. In this way, he could often be not fair in being right.

He had not ever liked Mary. Even as a girl she had looked at him and seen him in a way he could not abide. He had wanted a better family, as he put it, and now in her condition there was no reasoning with him. "Trash, excrement, don't even bring her name here," he shouted. "We will bring back the dowry and have her stoned, I have spoken already to the rabbis. I knew you would come back. You have pride! You have honor! I knew you would come to your senses. She will be dead. We will have our honor and you can have Sharon. Do not be a fool. No, no, say nothing, go to your room and think and in the morning we will go to the rabbis together, she will be stoned, and it will be done."

I said nothing. He had completely overwhelmed me and overpowered me as he always had. He was right as he always was. I went to my room and I did think of it.

I was home. My uncle would arrange it all. I would have a good life. A life without shame and dishonor; a life with this family and Sharon, the daughter of a prosperous merchant. Why not?

All children are given by God. Certainly this one was no more special than any other. In fact, far less so, it was a muzarim, a bastard, filthy, not fit to step into temple. What was I doing thinking of marrying into this mess?

How could I shame my uncle who had been so good to me? All of this and more circled in my head. Difficult decisions are never straight ahead, they circle and twist and wind. I did not sleep. I walked outside. Above me, the strange star and its light filled the sky. It was the star and my memory of my dream that helped me decide.

Outcast

I went to my uncle. I did not know what I would say until I said it.

"I love Mary. I want her to be my wife. I am the child's father, God gave us this child."

Spitting in rage my uncle was like a stricken cobra. He rose up out of his chair, struck me down and kicked me.

"Leave this house," he was screaming, "never enter here, you want to father a bastard and marry a whore, you are now a homeless bastard yourself. Speak no more to me ever again. I will have you both stoned."

So it was with a bloody mouth and a carpenter with no work or tools that I would come back to Mary.

Bloodied, I went to the well and washed and drank, while around me the people I grew up with pointed and whispered. I began to feel the pain and shame that Mary must have felt all these months—the lonely hurt of one outside. I walked without looking at them to Mary's house. Her mother greeted me with warmth and kindness. I have never forgotten this.

She told me Mary was washing clothes.

I saw her first kneeling by the stream.

The white water bubbled and frothed around her.

Her voice was laughing in a song.

Mary's eyes opened wide as she looked across the stream and saw me.

She rose to her feet, the sun behind her.

As she raised her arms to smooth her dark hair, droplets of water formed a circle of sparkling brightness all around her.

For just a moment, the world was alight with her smile.

I will remember her always in that moment before she crossed the stream to me in a halo of golden water and rainbow, as though the angel stood behind.

She could not have known whether I had come to love her or to stone her.

We stood just looking.

I reached with both of my hands to her

I sank to my knees and held her waist.

"I am sorry, I shall never strike you again. Forgive me, be my wife, you are my life."

Against my cheek, I felt her swollen belly.

Here, too, I said "I am sorry child,

I will be your father.

I will never leave you."

Mary came to her knees before me.

Her hands touched my cheeks, my broken nose, my swollen lips, my tears.

"My beloved," is all she said as she kissed me.

Then I learned that forgiveness and acceptance fills your arms and your heart and that the need for righteousness and revenge is only a bitter endless thirsting.

We walked up our hill, to our place under the trees looking out at the sea.

3

Acceptance or Denial

Joseph has traveled full circle in coming down from the mountaintop where he began his story to standing reunited with Mary looking out over the sea.

Swiss psychologist Carl Jung described a marriage as a circle with the man on one side looking across at the woman and the woman on the other side looking across at the man. In this circle, you are only able to see what is visible across from your own side of the circle, and this is what you take to be all of reality. The part that you cannot see, your partner does see, and she takes that to be all of reality. Thus, the only way to know the full circle of reality is to trust and believe in your partner, which is difficult, to say the least, since she is describing and experiencing a reality that you do not even know.

When he first walks down the mountain full of rage and disbelief, Joseph has no sense of the reality that Mary is trying to tell him about. The long process of believing and trusting and learning about reality, faith and consciousness has not yet begun on the mountain. He cannot believe

Mary and consequently cannot see or believe what she knows to be true. He leaves her behind, broken and bleeding on the ground. With one blow, he has broken their trust, their innocence and their bond. Joseph has great courage in telling this part of his story. He shows us that there is no place for this kind of behavior in a relationship and that he remembers and is ashamed even at the end of a long life at what he did in his anger and ignorance. He is trying to teach us the lessons of what to do with the inevitable tensions of relationship. He is trying to tell us that we must make a safe place in the home for the relationship and for every child.

As we know, one of the qualities of the World of Two is tension. Mary and Joseph have extraordinary tension. At first, Joseph reacts violently. By striking Mary, he destroys their innocence and their trust. He is not ready for the ordeal of relationship. He is outraged at the loss of his perfect life. He had expected his life and relationship to be one of all gain, to be predictable. He planned a relationship of profit, not of sacrifice and loss. He cannot bear to see Mary anymore. All he sees and feels is his own pain and his own loss of status and prestige. In his own pain, all he can think of is to hurt her.

As he stumbles off the mountain and then into the darkness he feels no acceptance, only rejection.

He thinks of ways to bring back his reputation, his honor, his picture of himself. His hurt and loss are all encompassing. He cannot see anything around him. He is in his own world. He simultaneously experiences the shattering of his World of One and his World of Two, and is thrust violently into the World of Three.

The World of Three

In the World of Three the most tension, the most pain and the most anguish exist. Here in the World of Three Joseph has to deal with fate, love, death, birth, mystery, faith and God. He is now in the midst of forces beyond the knowing of man. He is thrown adrift in the great currents of destiny that are far beyond his control and beyond his understanding. As he walks off the mountain and into the desert, he is on the Road of Soul.

The Road of Soul

The Road of Soul and the World of Three are synonymous and a stage that every father will enter. There is no escaping it. Born rich and privileged or down and out, life will bring everyone to their knees. On the Road of Soul there is pain and suffering, loss and difficult choices. Here lie all the great and mysterious questions. Why are we born? Why are we here? Why did I meet you and fall in love? Why did this child die? Where is God? Here in the World of Three are the unanswered questions. This is the world of great beauty and wisdom; the world of creativity, art, vision, ritual and metaphor. Poetry and narrative story are here. Tension in this world is so great as to be unbearable. It can literally destroy a person. Yet, this is the place of healing and redemption. The great issue in the World of Three is fate or destiny.

Joseph tries to deny and reject his destiny. He goes blindly out into the desert. He is in a dark mood, and he is in the dark in terms of enlightenment. He is beaten down by his own bullheadedness, his own unseeing and his own rage in the form of robbers along the road. He is able to hurt them, but in the end he is left crippled and naked to face the light. It is possible he was simply seeking oblivion. We can as men reject that we are fathers. We can run and hide, but there are consequences. We have already seen the statistics that show the consequences of fatherlessness for our society. We can deny the importance and the need of our children for fathers and as a society be beaten down and left crippled.

Wa iaomer Elohim iehi-aor, wa-iehi-aor.[1]
[And God said, "Let there be light," and there was light.]

Kahlil rescues Joseph, but not before he suffers the torment of being burned by the light. In the burning light, he loses consciousness and then a part of him dies. When he awakens, it is to see the kindness of Kahlil. He awakens to a new consciousness. He slowly is restored and he slowly builds acceptance of himself and of possibly returning to Mary and perhaps becoming the father of the child that Mary carries. This does not happen all at once. It occurs over time. His dignity and his self-esteem are restored in building the small house in the garden. It is important that all men find their own small house to build.

Kahlil is a gifted mentor and he creates a situation in which Joseph becomes a teacher in showing Kahlil how to be a carpenter. In the building, Joseph slowly becomes restored, and he builds a friendship. The friendship allows Joseph to see and hear himself. A friend allows a man to test his strengths and to show his weaknesses. A friend is essential, and many friends are a real richness. If they are real friends, they support each other's relationships and help

---

1. Douglas-Klotz, 40.

each other find the way along the soul road.

While Joseph Campbell viewed marriage as a religious exercise and sacrament, another of his ideas was that of the Heroic Journey. He tells us we all make that journey. Unlike the distorted American myth of the lone hero making his way over all obstacles to the top, the true Heroic Journey is one that often begins at the bottom after a fall. Down in the pit there is no way up or out by yourself. Every man needs help. It is in accepting help that the journey begins its ascent to another level of consciousness and understanding. The lone father is not a strong father. Fathering is a difficult and perilous journey and is done well with the help of other men.

In today's world we are often without uncles, grandfathers and older men to mentor and guide us. Too often, there is no other man to talk to about how to answer the difficult tasks of fathering and being a husband. Joseph is very clear that the way to strength in a man is through friendship with other men. Kahlil is a very important figure in his story. Kahlil is crucial in Joseph's finding the stage of acceptance in becoming a father. Fathers can help fathers. In the Norwegian National Fathering Project, mentor fathers were taught how to lead groups for new fathers. The men really helped each other, not only with newborns but also with fathering older children and teens. We will see how important Kahlil's friendship was in Joseph's fathering.

After Kahlil has helped Joseph mend his bones, his self-esteem and his spirit with his own loving kindness and acceptance, Joseph sees the strange and magnificent star. You might recall that a similar light surrounded him on the mountaintop when Mary told him about the child. At that time, he was unable to hear her or to see any of the light. After seeing the star and going to bed, he is visited by a great dream.

The Dream

Wa-iara Elohim aeth-ha-aor chi tob,
wa-iabeddel Elohim bein ha-aor w'bein ha-hoshe'ch.
[And God saw the light, that it was good:
and God divided the light from the darkness.][2]

According to Neil Douglas-Klotz, the ancient word *aor* refers to "all varieties of light, intelligence and elemental energy; everything that is enlightening or that produces joy, happiness, and grace."[3] The light from the star and the light Joseph sees in his dream is light sent from God. The light is the essence of elemental energy. The light burns through Joseph as when he was in the desert but this time the light is enlightening, bringing happiness and grace. In Aramaic the old phrase *iehi aor wa iehi aor* can be translated to mean "that which is created initially in a vision draws the present reality into existence in accordance with that vision."[4] What this means for Joseph is that the vision in his dream is a sacred one that literally brings into reality that which he dreams.

In this first great dream Joseph experiences again his own rage, violence, denial and his love of his own pride in the burning light. Covered in scorpions and dying of thirst he experiences the denial of faith, the denial of his own love of Mary. He also must experience faith in God in the form of the

---

2. Douglas-Klotz, 42.
3. Douglas-Klotz, 42.
4. Douglas-Klotz, 42.

angel. He has a choice in that strange clear light. He can come
forward towards faith, love and forgiveness, and find awareness and faith in Mary and the child; or he can stay consumed
with his thirst for pride and his own self-righteousness.

In his dream, Joseph makes the difficult choice. He steps
forward, is healed by cooling waters, accepted into the light
and forgiven. The Road of Soul is not easy. Making the decision of mature relationship is not easy for any man and neither
is making the decision to accept fathering. As we see in the
story, once a decision is made, it does not suddenly make
everything all right. A vow, a promise, a decision is made of
words and intent. The fulfillment requires action, will and
faith repeatedly.

God might send a vision, a dream or an inspiration, but you
still have to live from that vision or dream day by day to bring
it to fulfillment. Simply to stand up one day at church or any
place of faith and say "yes" is commendable but it does not
make the rest of life easy. Indeed, it likely will make life
harder for now comes the hard road of the daily practice of
prayer, faith and action. The same can be said for fathering. It
is easy to say, "Yes, let's have a baby." When the child comes,
then comes the day-to-day hard road of the daily practice of
fathering. It is something learned and earned.

Joseph says goodbye to his friend Kahlil not expecting to
see him again. He has had a great dream and is clearly on the
road of the soul but he still is naive. He believes that he can
simply go back and start where he left off. The light has
touched him and will draw him toward his destiny but he cannot yet fully see.

Joseph takes the first step in making the vision of his

dream come true. He must cross the water. He travels by sea, and when he arrives, he finds out immediately that life is not going to be easy. He is again tempted by his pride and ego to go a way other than the soul road. The way between the light and the darkness is repeatedly offered to him. Joseph's uncle has all the righteous answers, and puts enormous pressure and temptation on Joseph to take the easy road. Joseph is truly tempted. Fortunately, he has the light of the star to remind him of his way. He makes the choice for Mary and the child. In making his choice, Joseph becomes the rejected and the outcast from his family. His beating by his uncle is symbolic of stepping outside the bonds of expectation again.

Mary

Joseph has returned home, but not to simply start over as he thought he could. He is a man without home or work or status when he goes to Mary. He has little in terms of the World of One but he is on the road of the soul and rich in love and spirit in the World of Three when he again sees Mary.

When Joseph looks across the stream and sees Mary in a halo of water droplets, it is again another instance of the vision of his great dream coming true. He is going toward heart awareness and acceptance.

Ethphatah! Be Opened!

They brought Isho'a a man who could not speak or hear,
asking that he lay a healing hand upon him.
Isho'a took the man aside, so the crowd could not see, and
placed his finger gently into the man's ears.
As they breathed together, Isho'a drew closer,

spat on the ground, and touched the man's tongue,
uniting his sensing self with the other.[5]

A VERSION OF MARK 7:32–35
FROM THE PESHITTA VERSION OF THE GOSPELS

The last time Mary and Joseph were together, he was a
man who could not speak or hear. He had not yet opened.
His ordeal in the desert, his restoration by his friend and
mentor, and the great spiritual awakening of his dream have
been his initiation to prepare him for marriage and family.
He is ready for the stage of acceptance. Will Mary accept
him?

Mary crosses the stream. This is a strong and strong-
willed woman. She does not know why he has come back—
perhaps it is to have her killed. He has hurt her and
abandoned her. A man can do no worse. She has already
entered the sacred, the World of Three, and she can see him
clearly. She can accept him and forgive him out of her love
and faith, accepting his promise that he will never do so
again.

Joseph drops to his knees and asks for her forgiveness.
This is not what macho men might see as a place of
strength, yet this is one of the strongest and most powerful
statements in the story. He is not just on his knees to Mary,
but to Jesus, to fatherhood, to faith and to God. He asks for
her forgiveness for striking her, for leaving, for not believing and for his own absorption in himself. Here he is doing
the work of the soul. Love and faith are stronger than his
own ego and pride. His faith and belief in Mary and her love
for him mean more than what others may think about him or

5. Douglas-Klotz, 87.

what he thinks others will think of him. He is strong enough to set aside his male pride and ego. In this humbling act is one of the great keys to successful relationship. John Mordechai Gottman's research on marriage has clearly shown that one of the most critical of relationship skills is that of apology and forgiveness. Within the offering of apology and the gracious receiving of apology is the essence of successful relationship. The inability or lack of this interaction in a relationship is a strong predictor of marital unhappiness and breakup.

In every relationship, there is disagreement, conflict and argument. In every relationship, there are things said and done all the time, big and small, that require reconciliation. If there is no ongoing process of apology and gracious acceptance of apology, then tensions remain and build, and bitterness and resentments grow. The way of Joseph in going towards reconciliation and forgiveness is a way all men can move toward healthy relationship and the road of the soul. It is a kind of emotional skill and intelligence that children learn from watching their parents live out their relationship. A father showing his child that he can apologize and listen is showing his child how to have a successful relationship.

On their mountaintop and together again, Joseph and Mary are hopeful. The great gift of love between a couple is that everything seems possible. Joseph is again looking forward to his plans for a wonderful life with his bride-to-be. His ordeal and initiation into family and fathering are only beginning.

The Night Road to Bethlehem

I remember how innocent and hopeful we were that day. Wanting everything to be all right, believing that our love would be something that my uncle and everyone in Galilee could see and care about as we did. In only a few days, it was clear how naive we were. My uncle's words poisoned the very air. We returned the bride price to my uncle. He burned all of it. We married, but only Mary, her mother and I were happy. The ignorance and rudeness and the whispers grew threatening. There was no work for me. I had bought tools with the money from Kahlil but no one would hire me knowing the wrath of my uncle would spread to them. We were lepers there. There was now talk of stoning both of us. As each week passed and the time for the child came nearer my uncle's anger grew with Mary's stomach and we knew we had to leave to find a place safe for us and the child.

It so happened that there was a reason and an excuse for us to leave. Caesar Augustus had decreed that all must register. Each must go to their own city for the census. I would have to go to Bethlehem. We told no one but Mary's mother that we were leaving.

We decided to go in the night to Bethlehem. A cousin of Mary's mother lived there. In Mary's condition, we walked slowly. The night was very cold with winds. We bundled in all the clothes we had. We left behind all that we had ever known and hoped for, and were only the two of us on that night road to Bethlehem. The stars made a brilliant carpet across the black sky, and the strange bright star seemed always above us as we came to the small inn of Mary's relatives.

When we first arrived at the inn in Bethlehem, we were greeted warmly. There were many travelers because of the census, and we shared lodging in the barn with the donkeys, cows and horses. We were comfortable, warm and safe, and so we were happy. Mary helped her mother's cousin, a gracious and generous woman, serve guests in the inn. I was asked to buy some wood and begin to frame more rooms to expand the inn. It was good work and it was good to be in a place where we were welcome.

The Birth of Jesus*

The day the child came, Mary's water broke just after the sunset. She began her labor on the fresh straw and blankets we had brought. As I waited, there came word of a rich Persian caravan. Shortly thereafter servants arrived saying that their masters were coming and to prepare the inn. Then came the first of many unexpected gifts. They gave us two beautiful rugs, saying, "These are for the birth of the child." The carpets were like those you would find in the home of a king. I took them into the barn for Mary and her mother and her cousin.

As I came back outside the journeyers were arriving. There were many guards as the robes of the travelers were very rich. I was astonished when the first man threw back the hood of his robe and I knew him. The proud tilt of his head and those dark

[*Translator's note: here I used the familiar modern language form rather than Isho'a.]

brown eyes were unmistakable. It was my dear friend Kahlil.

He embraced me and then in answer to all my questions said, "Not everyday is a child born in this village and on this day only one." He pointed overhead where the great star blazed. "We have followed this star to this place to come to the blessing of the birth of this child." I was as amazed as if Moses himself had appeared and come to this simple inn for the birth of a baby. We heard then Mary's cries and the cry of a child. We all turned to the barn.

The whole procession entered the barn. I ran forward and fell to kneel next to Mary. She was tired, her face wet and flushed, but well and happy. In her arms was the baby. She reached out with the child in her arms.

Here, I confess, my heart was still cold. I had taken Mary back, but my manhood and pride had not really wanted this child. I looked down and, God forgive me, I did not know if I wanted this baby boy. I had decided to be a husband and to provide a home for this child, but to take it into my heart as my own? "Here is our son, that God has sent us," said Mary. Her voice shook a little for she knew well my old anger and she was afraid for the child.

I looked at the child, and here is my true memory. How could it be that the child, an infant, looked to me, right into me, and his arms and hands reached out for me? In that moment I reached out and cradled the baby. I brought its sweet-scented baby smell face to mine. Tears ran down my cheeks. As those tiny hands touched *my face I felt the last stone inside me break as if they had gone inside and touched my heart.*

"Jesus, Jesus, my little boy." I laughed and cried together with Mary, and never will I forget that first sweet baby scent next to my face, Mary's shining eyes, and the hands of baby Jesus holding tight to my hair, the little sounds of his voice in my ear.

So from the infant Jesus I was given the most important lesson of fathering and husbanding: the full circle of love and forgiveness and love again. There were other treasures and gifts that night, but none richer than what I received. Later my son taught many others this blessing, but I was the first.

The Silver Lamp, the Olive Tree and Two Gold Rings

Winter night
the wind sweeping cold out of the desert.
The black starry sky close and clear

the great star blazing in colors.
Its light making a night never seen before.

And for the child
in the manger
the men had brought
frankincense, incense and myrrh and more.

This, said the Persian in the blue silk robe,
is for the mother and father.
A small silver lamp for your marriage.
One side for each of you.
It is shining and beautiful you see.
Yet if you do not polish and care for your side
it will soon tarnish, darken.
You must keep it filled with good oil and care for the wick
to make the light.
You must always light the lamp when there is trouble, strife or
hurt between you.
In the soft yellow glow, pledge between you now to always talk
until you find the place of understanding. Honor this and the
lamp will hold you
together in its light of understanding.

This, said the man from Alexandria, is also for the two of you.
His robe was red and from the other side of the highest moun-
tain in the world.
When he moved it glowed against his black skin as though
there was light inside each thread.

He brought forth a vase in which lived a small olive tree.
This you must plant by your home.
It will give you shade in the heat
and its fruit will make oil for your lamp to warm the winters.
But you each must care for it and like the two of you

it will grow into its own shape made by the winds of God and give you shelter, food and warmth.

I have one of these for each of you, said the old man with yellow skin and eyes from far away.

His purple robe had the threads of light, figures of animals and a great dragon.

A small gold ring for love to wear each for the other.

To remember how precious was the moment you first truly saw one another.

To remember that what is between you lives only if you treasure it.

Above us the strange star sent out its light,

and around the child we sat and heard the stories of their journey.

In the glow of the silver lamp, Mary and I looked across at one another in wonder.

The night went on. . . . Each of the three visitors came forward to Jesus as if in the presence of a king, each knelt and gave the gifts they had brought, and each in turn held the baby. Last of all Kahlil, who had given frankincense, money for Mary and me, and the olive tree. He handed me a small cedar box. "For the house in the garden," he said. "There may come a time that you may need refuge or sanctuary for you and Mary and the child." It was the only shadow cast upon that night of light.

[Translator's note: Apparently authored by the writer of the narrative.]

We left Mary and Jesus to rest and went out under the stars to the caravan camp to celebrate. The sun rose and the strange star, too, blazed in the morning, creating a day when there were two suns. The old man said it was something foretold, but never seen before, making this a day like no other.

A Simple Life

For some time afterward, our lives were the simple life of a carpenter and his family in Bethlehem. There were many rumors about us. We lived close by the inn. Like the docks by the sea, an inn is a place where travelers and caravans bring the newest stories, rumors, jokes and news. The story of the exalted travelers from the East bringing gifts to the birth of Jesus of course was a story with wings. It flew throughout the land. By the time the story returned, it was said that a king had been born, a savior to save the people, a warrior god that all the world would worship, and that kings from all the world had already visited. Well, that story did not much look like Mary and me living in a barn so there were many stories of where the baby king lived.

Sadly, the story reached even the ears of Herod. By that time the story, like all stories, had grown, and Herod came to believe (he was insane) that this baby was a warrior god come to dethrone him, and that Persians were already bringing treasures of gold to dissident Hebrews to amass an army.

I was troubled to hear of Herod's obsession. I thought that perhaps this was also just a story that was exaggerated by the *telling, but soon there were more and more sightings of Herod's spies and soldiers throughout the land searching for the infant king. Fortunately, a barn was not the place the spies thought to look for a warrior god. My thoughts turned to what Kahlil and his esteemed friend had darkly warned at the birth. With every caravan and traveler, new stories came in that Herod had brought astrologers and magicians and soothsayers from near and far. They were telling him, of course, what he wanted to hear, that a warrior god messiah was coming to take his throne. Mary and I talked often, but we did not know what to do or where to go. I told her I had to walk and pray and went up a small mountain. She would know that I would be praying and not be troubled if I did not return until morning. I walked, and sat and prayed all night, and just before dawn I dreamed.*

The Second Dream

In the dream, I walked in darkest night with Mary and Jesus.

As we walked, the stars went out one by one like small lamps in a great wind. Behind us we could hear screaming and crying, the sounds of butchering and death. We were frightened and confused.

We hurried, but the shrieks and moaning grew closer and closer to us.

As the night darkened, as the sky emptied of all light, we did not know where to run.

Jesus began to bleed.

Our boy was dying.

Then came the light from the great star and the angel of God.

Then the angel stepped aside, and behind the angel was a gate.

I turned to look behind us.

The road we had traveled had turned into a river of blood moving in a huge wave. The angel said only, "Egypt" and opened the gate and we stepped through.

The gate closed behind us and we were in a garden, and safe.

I woke up and the light of the sunrise was blood red. I ran back down the hill to Mary. She heard my dream, and we both knew we had to leave. We left that night so no one would know where we had gone. We had only the money we had saved from Kahlil's gift but it was enough. We moved steadily toward Egypt and Alexandria.

Finally, we arrived at the gate in my dream. It was locked. The old servant remembered me, but would not let us enter since the master was away. I remembered the cedar box and the key. I opened the gate and the servant kneeled. Kahlil had left word that no one could enter the garden, save someone who carried the key. The keeper of the key would be the master of the garden and the garden house, and so we were saved by the dream sent by God and the wisdom and generosity of Kahlil.

Madness and Curses

It is with horror that I remember when we heard of the madness of Herod. Kahlil told me that one of his traders had witnessed the slaughter of the infants and every male child under the age of two. It was not just in Bethlehem, but everywhere Herod's power could reach. The streets of every village and city had run with the blood and the tears of the families of all of Judea. It ensured that we must stay in Egypt, for now not only was Herod our enemy, but certainly so were many of those that had lost their own child on account of ours. The suffering of all of the families due to Herod's bestial madness has troubled me and followed me all my life. My own cousins, nephews, and those of Mary died by the sword and were tossed like garbage. Of course when parents and families suffer, they often need to blame and we heard that many personally blamed Mary and me and our son who had not been found. One who was most angry was my uncle. His first grandchild had been slain with the others and we would suffer mightily for his curse, for he blamed our child for his misfortune. Fortunately, for now, we were safe. No one knew where we were or if we were alive.

4

Bonding and Connectedness and Boundaries

The Night Road to Bethlehem

On the mountaintop and together again, Joseph and Mary are hopeful. The great gift of love between a couple is that everything seems possible. Joseph soon finds that public condemnation does not care about love. He and Mary are outcasts among their own people and there is danger. They must leave behind their broken dreams and flee. They must make their own way as a marriage. Every couple will find the broken dreams of the night road. There will be lost jobs, lost friends, and even family who betray them. There may be car wrecks, houses burned or flooded, sickness, miscarriages and deaths. They will find themselves alone, with only each other to help them in the cold and the night.

The Birth of Jesus

The birth of the baby brings Joseph again into the mysterious World of Three. Here fate reunites him with Kahlil. The birth of the child brings gifts and an awareness of entering a life that they could not have imagined. It also brings Joseph face-to-face with his Self, his pride and his selfishness again.

For many men, their first child is a source of great pride about themselves. For other fathers, the child is an unwanted burden. For every man, the birth brings to reality and to flesh and blood something that they are never quite prepared for. They must make a choice to accept or not the role of father and the daily burden and effort required of a provider and protector. In addition, they must consider going even further along the development of fathering to the stage of bonding and connecting with their child.

For Joseph, the child is not his and therefore not about him. When the child is born, Mary reaches out, and Joseph is unexpectedly confronted again with himself. Joseph's honesty in relating this experience can help each man realize that before the baby arrives, and before we are confronted with the reality of the child, it is only an idea to be a father. Joseph or any man cannot automatically become a loving, nurturing father without first opening his heart to the child and making a commitment to truly be a father.

With Kit, Age 7, at the Beach

We would climb the highest dune,
from there to gaze and come down:
the ocean was performing;
we contributed our climb.

Waves leapfrogged and came
straight out of the storm.
What should our gaze mean?
Kit waited for me to decide.

Standing on such a hill,
what would you tell your child?
That was an absolute vista.
Those waves raced far, and cold.

"How far could you swim, Daddy,
in such a storm?"
"As far as was needed," I said,
and as I talked, I swam.[1]

WILLIAM STAFFORD

Joseph, too, has decided in that moment that he embraces the baby, that he will go as far as was needed. It is an important turning point for every father on the road of the soul. Being a father is sacrifice and doing what is needed. Being a father is caring and developing deep bonding and connectedness to your child. As a wise black father told his son in a special moment, "I can't give you everything you want, but I do everything I can to give you what you need."

A RESPONSIBLE FATHER (DADDY)

My father experienced a lifetime of social, psychological and economic disadvantages in the form of inadequate housing, poor medical care, job discrimination, improper nutrition and alienation in a hostile and racist white society in the Heart of Dixie (Alabama). However, he demonstrated a strong work ethic as a coping strategy to survive in spite of racial injustices

---

1. Robert Bly, James Hillman, and Michael Meade, eds., *The Rag and Bone Shop of the Heart* (New York: HarperCollins Publishers, 1992), 36.

and combated those injustices in his own individual way until he died of a stroke at the age of sixty-nine.

He was a powerful man with the physique of Hercules and feared no man—black or white. He was a proud and dedicated family man with a strong religious background. He was a praying man, a singing man. People would gather around and join in the singing and moaning of good old Negro spiritual hymns, such as: "Glory, Hallelujah"; "We Shall Overcome"; "Jesus on the Mainline"; "Ain't Gonna Let Nobody Turn Me Round"; "Jesus Is a Battle Light in the Time of a Storm"; "My Soul Say Yes Lord"; "Oh! Lordy, Lordy."

Although he was not an educated man by society standards and jobs were limited for "Negroes" or "colored," this did not deter him from his responsibility as a father and as a provider for his family of seven children and three foster-home children. I remember as a young African-American boy growing up in the South, my father looking me straight in the eyes, as he had taught me to do whenever I talked to anybody black or white, and saying, "Earnest, I can't give you everything you want, but with the help of the Lord I work hard to give you what you need." He made no apologies for what he could not give me.

He was a cotton picker. That was his identifying trademark. My father was well known in the communities by the labor that he had mastered. One of his greatest accomplishments and one that he was most proud of was when he received recognition as Cotton Picking Champion of Pike County, Alabama. He picked 714 pounds of cotton in one day—a record high! Masterfully and skillfully picking cotton earned him countywide respect and dignity that he so richly deserved.

I can remember the mornings of getting up early, well before sunrise, to go to the cotton field to pick cotton with my brothers and sisters without eating breakfast. My father's strategy was to pick the cotton early in the morning. There were two reasons: (1) the cotton and the cotton sacks would be wet with early morning dew during the first weigh-in at the cotton wagon; (2) after sunrise came the heat, and the shadeless cotton fields would be blazing hot with seemingly unbearable, shimmering waves of heat.

Before the other cotton pickers had even arrived, we would have picked several hundred pounds of cotton and were ready to eat some food at the first weigh-in. My father always said that we could pick more cotton by the first morning weigh-in than most families could pick all day. And, he was right!

At the first weigh-in and through the last you could hear the cotton pickers singing and moaning the old spiritual hymns from miles away across the fields. The spiritual moaning of melody and praises to open the windows of heaven and shower down blessings of hope and prosperity filled the air and rose up into the sky. Sometimes it seemed like the hymns, moans and heat filled the hours without ever a word being spoken. My father said that when they were singing and moaning the devil did not know what they were talking to the Lord about.

The strength of my father was in his powerful hands and his commitment to himself to provide for his family. As a young boy, I can remember placing both of my hands in the palm of one of his huge hands and imagining that some day my hands would be just as tough and powerful. I knew my hands could never be as tough as his hands because some of the joints of his fingers were permanently swollen hard. They had double-barked, discolored dark nails from being bruised by the keen-pointed, ripped cotton boll shells. The sharp points peeled the skin away from around his finger-nails and pierced the flesh of his fingers. Often, all down the row, the snowy white cotton would be smeared red with blood dripping from around his fingernails, as he gracefully picked the cotton from the open cotton boll shells and packed it methodically in his huge, personally designed eight-foot sack. My father could pick two rows of cotton faster than any challenger, man or woman. I can remember cotton pickers, black and white, coming from near and far just to challenge my father to a cotton picking race. It was to no avail because they found it just too difficult to keep pace even when they were picking just one row of cotton while he did two!

When the cotton gin machines put him out of work, my father took a dangerous job as a truck driver. Many nights I prayed for his safe return home because he was traveling around through the dangerous prejudice of the time deliver-ing animal feed for the Brundidge Feed Mill. He was often the victim of vicious racism during his travels. He also worked several other hand-me-down jobs to ensure that his family was sheltered, clothed and had food on the table all the time. I shared his off-duty times with him by going to church, farming the fields, raising hogs, chickens and cows, and going fishing and hunting.

We often went hunting for rabbits, raccoons, squirrels, possums or quail. Hunting wild game and birds provided food for us to eat. In my mind, it was not an experience shared for the sport of pursuing wild game or simply for the thrill of the chase, or the enjoyment of outdoor recreation. It was a matter of having meat to eat or not having meat to eat for that day and the next.

I remember one day my father and I went hunting with our black hound dog named Sussy. On this particular day, I shot a rabbit, and Sussy was with my father and so I had to go retrieve the dead rabbit myself. Normally, Sussy would retrieve the dead wild game, and she did it very well. When I found the rabbit, I picked it up and to my surprise the rabbit was still alive. As I held that rabbit in my hands, I could feel the warmth of its soft fluffy hair. It was shaking and trembling and the blood from the gunshot wound was dripping through my fingers.

When my father and Sussy arrived, I was still holding the rabbit in my hands. I was shaking and could barely breathe as I watched and felt the life pass from the rabbit I had shot. My father took the rabbit and placed it in the wild-game bag. With his twelve-gauge shotgun in one hand, he put his other arm around me, lifted me completely off the ground and gave me a big kiss on the jaw. As we were walking out of the hunting area he whispered in my ear, "Earnest, you don't ever have to go hunting again, if you don't want to."

My father was very important to me as a young African-American boy growing up in the South. He played a major role in the molding of my character and values, and in my own growth and maturity in becoming a father. He was a good father and an excellent role model.

Joseph's embrace of Jesus is the next stage of his initiation and transformation into fatherhood.

There is a profound moment in the touching between Joseph and Jesus. Joseph's heart is open and he accepts this child as his to love and care for. He goes beyond protector and provider to Stage Three—bonding and connecting. This can happen to any man of any age. This can happen to biological fathers and to stepfathers. It can happen to teachers, coaches, uncles and grandfathers. There are children everywhere reaching out for us, and they need us to come forward and be their fathers. How do we go beyond the old roles of father? How do we accomplish the bonding and build the connectedness of Stage Three and move to Stage Four fathering? Let us look to Joseph.

The Garden-House Years

It is good to remember those years when we all lived here together in this little house in the garden. Kahlil's home was near the sea and close by the great library of Alexandria. Kahlil's many friends had much work for me. Life was very good for Mary, our little son and me. It was a time of joy and learning for all of us.

The Great Library of Alexandria

Kahlil was a wise man and scholar. His associates were the great wise ones of the library of Alexandria. Kahlil inherited the role of Eratosthenes, the first keeper of the library and known as the most learned Greek in Egypt. He had been the keeper of the prophecies of Ancient Egypt, the knowledge of the Wise Men, the Magi, the Zoroastrians, Jews, the Gnostics, the Essenes and the others who kept the recollections of time. The knowledge that the Prince of Peace was to be reborn as a lamb was the prophecy that brought Kahlil to Bethlehem.[2] He had not known I was there, and it was a wonder to him that in finding a broken, bloody carpenter he had become so much a part of the destiny of our son.

Fathering

I should say now that my becoming a father was not always an easy thing. Jesus was a good baby but, as fugitives,

---

2. Gerald Massey, *Ancient Egypt: The Light of the World* (London: Richard Clay & Sons Ltd., 1907), 732.

we did not have the usual help of aunts and older cousins and grandmothers. Mary was again with child and often ill this time. There were many times that I was solely responsible for the care of Jesus. After I had mastered the art of diapers (made from the soft rushes from the river), and the use of oils and baths, my hard carpenter's hands learned gentleness and patience. It was in caring for the child that my love grew and grew for him. For men, the doing creates love. It does not make a man into a woman when he cares for a child; it makes a man a father. In doing this work, a man finds understanding and respect for the work that women do, as well as for the work of men. In doing this work, a man grows the heart bond that connects himself to his child. The connectedness of this early caring when the child is young lasts all the days of a man's life.

And so, in the work of caring for Jesus, my bond with my little boy grew as he did. Our son Jesus was a wonder and a joy, but of course, all parents say that. Jesus, however, seemed extraordinary in an almost indescribable way. He could speak as an infant. He could walk, it seemed, only a moment after he crawled, but he loved to be carried on my shoulder and my back.

Extraordinarily, and here I say something you could believe only if you witness it, he could understand anyone who spoke to him! At first you might think he was a child who paid close attention, nodding his head at the right times but only seeming to understand, but then he would respond in the language of who-ever spoke to him!

When Kahlil first took him to the Great Library, he would speak in the tongue of anyone who spoke to him. That is not to say he did not have to learn for he was, after all, a child. Nevertheless, he could speak and sound like a Greek, an Egyptian, a Roman, or anyone else he heard, and his understanding of languages grew so fast it was unbelievable. Even deeper than his understanding of words was his way of understanding people inside their hearts. Anyone who spoke with him felt themselves to be understood and deeply so. This way of being grew as he did. So it was that, as he grew older, anyone could speak with him and he would know them and they would know he understood them in their words and in their heart. He told me often that it was not special, but something we all could do if we really listened.

Kahlil commenced with teaching Jesus as soon as my child could walk. At first, it was from books and scrolls at Kahlil's house. Then came the first day we went to the Great Library.

We walked to Brucchium. It was a short stroll from the garden, in the northeast sector of the city and close to the palace. Courts, gardens and a zoological park surrounded it. It was as if the whole world was in this great library in the form of plants, animals, people and books gathered from everywhere.

At its heart was a great hall. The circulum, a domed dining hall, rose to the sky. It was filled with Egyptian glass that allowed colored light to flow through, and the beauty of the room and the light was a wonder. In the center on the upper terrace was an observatory. *Surrounding the domed dining hall were class-rooms where scholars came each day. Many were daily visitors, but thirty to fifty scholars were in residence who were permanently housed at the library.*

Kahlil told us it was Ptolemy I's great ambition to house all of the earth's known literature. Books were brought, bought and stolen from everywhere. There were many scribes and a school for training them. It was here that my son, and then I, learned to write and to make the Rota Code on which I write this story.

It was in the dining hall when he was still a small boy that Jesus was first able to join the scholars. A friend of Kahlil's, an Egyptian, came to greet us and Jesus spoke to him in his language. The man beside him exclaimed in Greek that this was a trick, but Jesus spoke to him in Greek and then to a Roman beside him. "The boy of the great star," said Kahlil when introducing him. From that time, Jesus spent a day each week at the library with the scholars and Kahlil.

Most days, he came with me to build things. He would help carry my tools. As he grew stronger, I began to teach him to be a carpenter. Like every boy, he would try the tools too soon. He was too small and the tools too big. He would use the hammer at the wrong time. He would want his work to be perfect and then would break things when they were not turning out the way he expected. He would smash them in frustration. He would want to quit and never try again. He would make joints that would not fit and become heartbroken, or blame the wood or the tools. I had to learn to go slowly, carefully and persistently. I was building a carpenter and helping to build a man. It was slow and careful work and often made for broken nails, splinters, cuts and tears. This too was a part of my fathering. I would stop the work and hold him while he cried. Then I would take out the splinter. I still recall seeing his big eyes filled with tears and looking only at me, as I carefully removed the splinter or mended the broken nail. I learned patience. I learned to take time to show him. When I remember those times working side by side with him, they are the treasures of my life. It is in standing and working and doing together that boys learn from their fathers how it is to be a man. The days often seemed long in summer, and we would lift a perfectly fitted window or door into place and our eyes would meet and his smile was the sun.

He grew strong and tall for his age. Always his mind grew and grew. The days at the library with Kahlil brought him knowledge of the entire world and the wisdom of all the wise men and women. He learned all of the names of God and all the forms of worship and believing. He learned all the ways of healing and medicine. When just a boy, he could somehow see what hurt in others and take it away with his words and his touch.

He was never just a boy with books and scholars.

Often Kahlil would search for Jesus for his lessons. He would find Jesus in the kitchen getting sweets from the cooks. He would find Jesus in the streets where the children from everywhere in the world played games from everywhere in the world. Jesus loved to *wander, and there were many times, to keep him safe, I had to limit what he could do and where he could go. He could not always do everything he wanted to do. A part of love is discipline. A child will not always like the boundaries or the discipline, but that is the way of real love. A father must protect his children by making the boundaries of safe and not safe, good and bad, and right and wrong.*

He loved to play. He would make games of everything and laugh and laugh. He was not afraid. He hated bullies and would rush in when anyone tried to push or harm someone smaller, and he suffered for it. For he often got the worst beatings from the rough ones for trying to defend the little ones. Nevertheless, he always came back and would befriend the bullies and stand up for them when he saw them hurt.

"I cannot help it," he told me when he was older. "I hurt when I see it and have to do something." When he began to learn the arts of medicine from the scholars, it was those who were sick and suffering that we could not pass without his stopping. Always he would ask Kahlil or myself for money and then give it to the beggars and the poor. Everything he learned he would teach to the poor and to the slaves he saw on the streets and the ship docks. He sometimes cried at night with his mother because the suffering he saw hurt him.

I started to wonder how he could live in this world, for he seemed to be too tenderhearted. He never got used to others suffering. He could not look away or harden himself to it. It was as if it was fresh and new to him each time he saw it. Mary would hold him like a baby as he sobbed about a slave he saw being cruelly blinded, deafened or whipped to death.

The Slave Galley

Once when Jesus was ten, he begged Kahlil and me to take him on board a Roman war galleon. He loved to see the big ships with their oars thrashing the waters white. We should have known better than to take him on board. As soon as we boarded, he wanted to go down to the galleys to see the men who made the ship sail. To see his face when he saw the slaves was agony. As you might know, these were no longer men.

Cruelty and hopelessness had turned them into vicious animals that would kill for a scrap of bread.

They were doomed and hopeless beasts.

They were slaves from the entire world who would never see home or loved ones again.

They would never again know any kindness.

They were all the colors of the world.

Yellow men, brown, black, red, gold- and red-haired men from strange, far-off places.

I tell you, I was afraid and wanted to take Jesus and go.

Any of them could have killed or strangled him with a chain.

When Kahlil and I walked down the stairs, it was like entering the house of the dead.

They turned and looked at us with eyes of death and hate.

Jesus walked down behind us.

They were still.

"I told you I would come," he said.

He spoke to each man in his own tongue from his homeland.

These lost men, for just a moment, were home again and safe.

They talked of snowy mountains, rivers with strange names, and fishing and games they played when they were boys.

They laughed as he sang a song or recited a poem with them.

As he washed them, bound their wounds and oiled their hands, their dead eyes came to life and the man who lived inside them spoke.

When Jesus rose to leave there was light in there.

One by one, he parted with saying:

"I will remember you."

His small arms hugged them as they would a lost older brother.

The galley master stood in silence when he saw that Jesus had healed the slaves' wounds. As we left, Jesus said to him, "And you know I will remember if they die kindly." It was only when we stood back on shore that my little boy turned to me and cried. He sobbed into my chest for those men he knew would die on those benches in their chains. He cried for a long time, and it was the first time I saw him cry blood. His own blood was in his tears as he wept for those men.

This incident greatly affected Kahlil. Though a kind man— he had already saved my life twice—he now saw the world through the eyes of a master. In that stinking, rotting death galley, his own eyes changed. From that time on, he took Jesus with him when he heard of a great ship of war coming to port. Together they would go into the bottom of the ships. Later, when we were old men, he said to me, "I learned everything I know of man, God, spirit and soul in the bottom of that ship in that afternoon. All the days of my life with the scholars and wise men in the library were only words."

With his mother, Jesus often went to the market. He could laugh and talk with the women as with the men. For many peoples, their women were like their animals. The beatings and pain these women suffered hurt him. He was proud that his mother went to the library with him and that she wrote as well as any scribe and knew mathematics and the ways of the stars. He loved her voice and the songs that she wrote. He had her independence, spirit, quick humor and laugh. He cherished her love for him as a treasure.

Traditions and Play

In the autumn, after the holy days, it was our tradition to go to our special place by the sea with the children. There are traditions in holy days and traditions in families. It was always important for me to have traditions with the children, to assure we always did certain things at certain times in certain ways. To put a child to bed with a story or song makes that time a blessing. To go to trees when they bear fruit and bring back a meal gives a family and a child some certainty in a world that is always changing, frightening and undependable.

I tried to make those traditional times with my children as sacred as holy days. No work, meeting or anything could interfere or become more important. The children could then depend on those times. I made sure I had separate traditions and times with each one of them so that they would know they were important to me in their own way. In this way, they did not resent or dislike the time I spent with the other. Most of all, they then enjoyed and loved the time we could have together, and for all of us the best was the trip to the sea in autumn.

The place we had found was a long day's walk. It was a place by the sea that only we knew. I had seen it from a ship. It was a lovely beach with white sand. Behind it was a spring, and some fine trees grew there for shade and fires. The fishing was very good, and we could swim, walk and climb. Often there were times we would all wrestle and play in the sand and in the water. I was always the great sea crocodile. I would chase them and catch them, and we would wrestle and fight. They would attack, punch, kick and jump on the poor crocodile with all their might. Even as they all grew stronger, they never grew tired of this simple but great game. It was the way they learned their own strength and learned how to control the violence and aggression that lives inside all people.

For Jesus and his brothers, James and John, this was their most special time. Some times Kahlil and his sons would join us, but most times, we went alone. It was a week of camping, stories, walking, talking and caring for each other.

The Death of John

In the year when Jesus was twelve, just before his thirteenth birthday, we planned our trip to the sea. Sadly, the day before we were to leave, John broke his ankle. Kahlil and Jesus set it easily but there was no chance he could walk on it all day and make the hard climb down to the beach. He was heartbroken. We decided to go. Just Jesus and James and me this time and then we would all go again as a whole family after the first of the year after the celebration of the holy days and Jesus' birthday.

We all agreed, and John goodheartedly and bravely smiled as we left him, his mother and little sister and started to the sea. We all missed John. At every meal we said a prayer for him, and at almost everything we did, Jesus and James would talk of what John would have done or said if he were there. For Jesus it was like a piece of him was missing. John had always followed him everywhere. Most older brothers would have found this a nuisance, but there was something special and unspoken between Jesus and John. There was a joy in each other for the other's life. John tried in every way to be like his brother. He even walked and talked like him. There was also something special between Jesus and James, and after what happened during the next few days there would always be even more. On the last night, we made our fire early. We were watching the sun set in that easy tiredness that comes from swimming and fishing, sea and sun. Jesus suddenly jumped up and cried out, "Oh my father, no, no!" and we were all afraid.

"We must go home now," he cried.

We packed our things and began the journey home in the dark, for I trusted these premonitions. Jesus ran home and arrived well ahead of James and me with all of our packs.

Around the garden and the garden house were gathered Kahlil's servants. I entered the house and there were Mary, little Esther, and Kahlil and his wife and sons. Lying bloody on the carpet, white and with the mask of death, was John. Bent over his chest was Jesus, silently crying, tears streaming down his face. His shoulders shook and trembled. He held John's bloody hands in his.

The wounds were terrible. His face, neck and hands were hacked and slashed in many places. I put my arm around Jesus, and the other around Mary. James knelt next to me, crying and touching John's hair.

"They thought he was me, Father. They thought he was me, and they killed him," cried Jesus.

"We were coming back from the market," said Mary. "He begged to get out and he was walking so well with his crutch. We got something to eat, and then went to watch the sunset because he knew it was the last night and could feel he was watching it at the beach with all of you. They must have followed us from the market. They were your uncle's men. They jumped at John and me. He saw them coming and he blocked the sword from my head with his crutch. The sword went right to his throat, and as he fell they hacked at him shouting, 'Kill the muzarim. Kill the false messiah.' Then they turned on me as I tried to stop them but *one of Kahlil's men came running with his sword drawn. They turned and ran shouting out your uncle's name and that Jesus was dead." She fell against me sobbing.*

I could see the tormented pain in Jesus as he heard this. "He died for me," he whispered, "and this is true." I saw his tears turning to blood. As they fell on John, the terrible wounds from the swords disappeared and his body was whole and unmarked. "Dear, dear brother," he whispered, "your spirit is gone, already you are with my Father." Then the sound of his sorrow and his mother's and all of those who loved our John filled the room. All but my own voice resounded. I sat in pain, but without tears.

We buried our son according to custom, and I could not rest. My anguish and my hatred grew inside of me each day. While I worked, I thought of revenge. I could not lie by my wife at night and listen to her tears for her little boy. I turned over all the work I was doing to a friend. Privately, I arranged to return to Galilee where I would murder my uncle and the men who had done this to me. My heart burned for it.

5

Developing Personal, Moral and Spiritual Intelligence

When they flee to Egypt, Joseph's life again dramatically changes. Until this point in his story, Joseph speaks of becoming a father before he has actually done any caretaking. The early part of becoming a father for Joseph is Stage One, Stage Two and his own coming of maturity to become a father. He learns to establish a relationship, make a commitment, and be able to listen to and hear his wife. These are critical parts of becoming a father. In his own way then, a man goes through a pregnancy of sorts. He goes through his own passage and becomes ready physically, emotionally and spiritually for the commitment of accepting the role of father. Then he must become another kind of father.

Fathering

Joseph talks openly of his becoming a father by doing the fathering. Again, there is sacrifice. He must relocate to provide protection to Jesus. Again, his own spiritual practice and faith provide him direction. He must flee to Egypt to protect the destiny of his child. He goes to Alexandria where he finds sanctuary with his friend Kahlil. Here he learns what fathering is. He speaks of his bond with the boy, a bond that grew from the caretaking.

In the Norwegian National Fathering Project, it is clear to see the bonds that develop when fathers do the caretaking of their infants and small children. Men are excellent caretakers. They are excellent nurturers. One of the most important lessons for men in the fathering programs in Norway and in the United States is to simply realize how very important they are for their children. In *USA Today*, an article cited how paternity leaves were increasingly popular and that in any given month there were about six thousand fathers on paternity leave, double the number from 1994. Saigon reported that the number of men now taking leave was small but growing and that more companies are starting to offer leave, usually noncompensated, for men as well as company-sponsored fathering/parenting programs.[1]

A critical aspect of the project was the decision of the Norwegian government to provide new fathers a paid three-week paternity leave to stay home from work to care for newborns. The intention of the government was to strengthen family life. The belief was that early bonding with their children was important for fathers and that this emotional bond was something that would last a lifetime for father and child. The intention of the Fathering Project is that even in case of divorce the father will stay involved with his children and that the child will not suffer the pains

1. Stephanie Armour, "Dad Is Job One: Paternity Leaves Increasingly Popular," *USA Today*, 23 February 1998, sec. B, p. 1.

of fatherlessness. In these circumstances there is a development of more fathers taking more care of their children. Five years ago, less than 5 percent of Norwegian fathers had a leave from work in conjunction with the birth of a child; today more than 75 percent take leave.

Fathering groups are a means of supporting fathers' deeper involvement in childcare and parenting. The Norwegian Fathering Project acknowledges that children need fathers, and that better quantitative and qualitative contact is necessary. As mentioned earlier, Norwegian fathers do not know about their own importance, especially not as to the needs of the youngest children. Fathers also do not trust their own contributions and their childcare skills. However, we want to emphasize that within a family with children, there is another kind of work for men—a very important type of work—the real work of fathering. Joseph's story shows us how a father was essential in Jesus' life. He shows how essential fathers are to raising their children.

Even if not the principal caregiver, the father can be what has been called the crucial third party, "who assists, encourages, spells off, gives status to, and expresses admiration and affection for the person caring for and engaging in joint activity with the child."[2]

The Norwegian Fathering Project has shown that during the time when the father is operating as principal caregiver, it is important that he be given the same kind of admiration,

2. U. Bronfenbrenner, "Discovering What Families Do," in David Blankenhorn et al., *Rebuilding the Nest: A New Commitment to the American Family,* (Milwaukee, Wisconsin: Family Service American, 1990), 33.

encouragement and status as the mother. In the Norwegian fathering groups, fathers are taught by mentor fathers such nurturing and caring skills as holding the infant, diapering, bathing and feeding. The men appreciate this knowledge and become proud of their abilities. It eliminates the shame and embarrassment some men report of being teased by family members when they do not have these skills. Many men had reported that this kind of teasing had "turned them off and away from doing the nurturing and caretaking even though at some level they had wanted to." Fathers can be fine caretakers when given the opportunity.

The fathering groups in Norway are the beginning of a process to have stronger fathers with resultant stronger families by providing fathers with tools to assume a stronger role in the lives of their children. According to a recent research project in Norway, 90 percent of younger fathers do not want to be the way their own fathers had been. It appears that the fathering groups can improve both the child rearing and the relationship of father and child. Fathers who go into the groups do change. A Swedish project showed that fathers who did engage in sharing care for their infants were a lot more active in interactions with their children through childhood and adolescence.

The Great Gift of Time

Joseph spends a great deal of time with his son. He cares for him as an infant and small child. He bathes and clothes him.

Joseph's story provides us with a model for ways of fathering. When his child is very young he provides nurturing and caretaking through feeding, bathing and clothing. These are bonding experiences for Jesus and Joseph. As the boy grows, Joseph takes him to work with him. He begins to teach him how to use tools and the basic skills of being a carpenter. He is bringing his child into the adult world in a safe and controlled way and showing him the abilities that are needed to live in the adult world. He is spending time with his child side by side. Like it or not, children measure caring in terms of time. Fathering takes time.

James Hill's Story

James Hill, seventy-four, is the father of three daughters and is a loving and devoted grandfather. A pilot in World War II, James has been a Sunday school teacher in his Methodist church for over twenty-five years. He has a quiet strength, great warmth and dignity. His story is a poignant one, looking back from the vantage point of age and wisdom.

WHAT IT MEANS TO BE A FATHER

When the youngest of my three daughters was in college, she wrote a short essay for a class she was in. The title was "Daddy." In the essay, she told of some of her experiences with me, both as a young child and as a maturing teenager.

My daughter was very complimentary in what she wrote. I will always remember it. However, the message I received from what she wrote troubled me. I have thought of it many times over the years. The memorable and important events she mentioned should have been usual and frequent occurrences, not just isolated highlights.

I have thought so many times of all that I had missed over the more than twenty years that the girls lived at home. Perhaps more important, what they had missed. In many ways, I was an absentee father. Of course, I was home every night, but often after they were already asleep. Certainly, I was on hand for all emergencies. I could usually attend all special occasions such as music recitals, father-daughter banquets and graduations.

Nevertheless, was I really there, or was my mind on my business? Was I really involved with their lives as a father should be and as I now wish I had been?

There never was a real family vacation. I could never be away from my business for long. A long weekend to a nearby place of interest was the norm. There was never a time when the family could explore new and interesting places together. Just our family, together for two weeks, would have given me more insight into their lives.

Of course, I had excuses (not real reasons). Being self-employed in the retail business, I worked ten to twelve hours a day, six days a week, all the time they were growing up. My work was necessary; after all, it was for them! I had to provide food, shelter, clothing and the extras. Another excuse I used for not being involved more fully is that I told myself that they were girls and that their mother was the "main parent" because she understood them better than I did. There was not enough time to do those special things with the girls that they wanted to do with me individually and together.

What were their real interests as they were growing up? I don't know. What were some things that troubled them? What was "bugging" them? Perhaps I would have helped them understand how they were feeling. As a father, as head of the family, I had responsibilities, including providing them with material well-being, and teaching and role modeling moral and ethical standards for them. However, I know there was more. I missed being a part of their lives. I was not a part of the experiences they were having growing up. I was not there to answer questions, offer ideas, stimulate interest in life and help them find direction.

Fortunately, all three girls have become honorable, educated, productive, contributing members of society. Any father would be as proud of them as I am. However, they have had more than their share of disappointment and heartache. I believe that, if I had been more available, many "bad times" may have been avoided. At the very least, I am sure my own life would have been much richer.

Now well past the biblical threescore and ten, I look back over my life with few regrets. The only one that really troubles me is that I made some poor choices in deciding what was the most important use of my time during those precious twenty-five years when my girls were at home and I was not there.

Special Time

Joseph knows to take time with all his children. An old friend, who is a child psychologist, once told me that one of the keys in his own fathering was in telling each of his three children that he would be setting aside a special time to be with them individually. There were the "all together times" but also, always, a special time set aside to be with one child. This special time let his children know that they were each unique, they were each special to their father and that they did not have to fight with the others for attention and time. Joseph does this in his story.

Another important lesson Joseph gives Jesus is that in taking Jesus to work with him, he is modeling and teaching the skills of making a living. This is not simply about making money. It goes much deeper than that, in that Joseph is showing Jesus how to gain the skills and tools of being a human being and to make a good life. That is the work of fathering.

Along the way, Joseph learns. He learns patience. He needs to learn to see the child's clumsiness. He shows Jesus how to use the too-large, too-sharp, sometimes dangerous tools of life building. Sometimes Jesus gets hurt. Sometimes Jesus is frustrated and angry or reckless. This is when Joseph does something very special; he becomes an emotional coach for his child.

Emotional Coaching

Joseph helps the boy to understand his emotions and his hurts. In doing this, he takes on the role of the emotional coach. He coaches the boy about how to deal with anger, pride, temper and passion, frustration and discouragement. The coaching of the control and use of emotions is a vital role in fathering. It is one of the most important ways to initiate and guide a child into becoming a well-balanced human being. It is one of the great and necessary gifts passed on from father to child in each new generation. This is wonderfully described in the poem, *The Gift*.

The Gift

To pull the metal splinter from my palm
my father recited a story in a low voice.
I watched his lovely face and not the blade.
Before the story ended, he'd removed
the iron sliver I thought I'd die from.

I can't remember the tale,
but hear his voice still, a well
of dark water, a prayer.
And I recall his hands,
two measures of tenderness
he laid against my face,
the flames of discipline
he raised above my head.

Had you entered that afternoon
you would have thought you saw a man
planting something in a boy's palm,
a silver tear, a tiny flame.

Had you followed that boy
you would have arrived here,
where I bend over my wife's right hand.

Look how I shave her thumbnail down
so carefully she feels no pain.
Watch as I lift the splinter out.
I was seven when my father

took my hand like this,
and I did not hold that shard
between my fingers and think,
Metal that will bury me,
christen it Little Assassin,
Ore Going Deep for My Heart.
And I did not lift up my wound and cry,
Death visited here!
I did what a child does
when he's given something to keep.
I kissed my father.[3]

LI-YOUNG LEE

Emotional coaching provides the emotional groundwork for every child's later relationships. The importance of this cannot really be overstated in building a successful life in work, play, friendships and intimate relationships. As illustrated in the poem, and by Joseph, the skilled father passes on the ability to the child. The emotional coach provides interpretation of emotions and situations, he provides guidance in what to do and how to do it, and at all times shows how to be a morally, emotionally and spiritually intelligent person as an emotional coach.

Emotional and Behavioral Boundaries

The coach provides boundaries of behavior. Children naturally push to find their limits. It is one way in which they grow up. Watch a toddler in the park. Usually, in a new place they will wander just a few steps away from the parent in

---

3. Robert Bly, James Hillman, and Michael Meade, eds., *The Rag and Bone Shop of the Heart: A Poetry Anthology* (New York: HarperCollins Publishers, 1992), 137–138.

exploring their new environment. Then they will go a little further and a little further, come back to touch and gain reassurance from the parent, and then back again to stretch the boundary. As they grow, these boundaries grow, and they often push farther than their own judgment and awareness can safely take them. In Joseph's story, there are times he must be a good parent and place boundaries and restrictions on the growing Jesus. Joseph has an adult perspective on what is safe, what is appropriate, when to go and when not to go further. Of course, the child will resist and not be happy. The boundaries are always being pushed on and being pushed back. This is the art of fathering: firmly placing boundaries, yet understanding that as the child grows, the child inevitably pushes back the restrictions in testing his or her own strength and judgment. Eventually, in adolescence and early adulthood, children break through into their own selfhood and full responsibility for their own life.

Emotional Coaching in Play

Joseph provides an essential emotional coaching role in playing with his children. All children love to play. One of their favorites is to play at fighting and wrestling. In this basic and simple kind of play (which is often done with fathers) are profound lessons. In this kind of play is learned the important lessons of how to control strength, aggression and violence. When they are small, children can wrestle and fight with all of their strength against their father. They can go to the limit with their violence and aggression. They can experience deep emotions in the context of this play with someone who can wholly contain it. The father provides a safe place to contain these potentially dangerous emotions. A child can push with all the power of their emotions and their physical strength. They learn their own strength. They learn with the emotional coaching of their father how to control themselves physically and how to control their emotions. They can see modeled for them how to use gentle force, how to hold back and control one's temper, how to play hard and yet not to harm.

As children grow older and stronger, they learn that they too can hurt and harm and that to keep the play going they must also learn to hold back and control their emotions and their strength. A friend, who is the father of two teens, tells me that now that the boys are strong enough to really hurt him, they make the rules of the wrestling and roughhousing. When they were young, the two boys could hurl themselves off furniture from all directions, jump on his back and shoulders, and punch and hit as they wanted. Now they know they are strong. They can harm and hurt their father. Now they know that, just as their father once had to control himself and his strength, they have to control themselves in order for the game to go on. He has passed on his own ability to control violence, aggression and emotions to his sons.

Emotional Coaching Develops Personal, Moral/Spiritual Intelligence

After all is said and done, what are the results of emotional coaching? One of the most important consequences is raising a child who has developed a capacity for personal intelligence. Personal intelligence is a part of every child's mental equipment. It exists as a potential that can be educated and enhanced. Brain researcher Dr. Howard Gardner and his colleagues at the Harvard Project on Human Potential developed the concept of personal intelligence. He wrote an important book in 1983 called *Frames of Mind*.[4]

Gardner studied all kinds of intelligence and all different kinds of human genius from piano prodigies to math wizards to superstar athletes. Out of his work with the extremes of the intellectual continuum, he believed that there was scientific evidence to support his contention that there were actually distinct and different kinds of intelligence.

In his book, Gardner lists several types of intelligence. They are:

1. Linguistic intelligence
2. Musical intelligence
3. Logical-mathematical intelligence
4. Spatial intelligence
5. Bodily-kinesthetic intelligence
6. The personal intelligence[5]

An example of exceptional linguistic intelligence would be Shakespeare or Toni Morrison or poet Pablo Neruda. Bach or Mozart or Duke Ellington are examples of musical intelligence. Albert Einstein or Stephen Hawking are prime representatives of logical-mathematical intelligence. Spatial intelligence can be seen in the work of Picasso, Leonardo da Vinci and Rodin. Bodily-kinesthetic intelligence is readily understood by observing those as gifted as French mime Marcel Marceau, Olympic skater Tara Lipinski, the dancer Baryshnikov or basketball player Michael Jordan. Examples of the personal intelligence

4. Howard Gardner, *Frames of Mind* (New York: Basic Books, 1983).
5. Gardner, 239.

would include Gandhi, John F. Kennedy and great teachers like
John Wooden or Marva Collins.

While each of the above is representative of someone particularly gifted in one of the multiple intelligences listed by
Gardner, they also represent the superior development of
skills, technique, and many years of training and practice in
their respective areas of expertise. In Gardner's view, an
intellectual competence is made up of a "set of skills" that
help us solve problems and difficulties. It is evident then
that emotional coaching is essential to developing the sets
of skills that make up personal intelligence.

The Personal Intelligence

According to Gardner, the personal intelligence is the
most mysterious, least understood and most important of all
of the intelligences. The personal intelligence is divided
into two parts: the interpersonal and the intrapersonal. Each
part has distinct kinds of emotional and psychological
skills.

Intrapersonal Intelligence: Being Smart About Yourself

Intrapersonal intelligence is concerned with the development of the internal aspects of a person. It is concerned with
the crucial skills of being aware of, sensitive to, and effectively being able to discriminate between our feelings,
thoughts, emotions and awarenesses. Personal intelligence
means being able to draw upon our feelings to understand
and guide our behavior. It is through emotional coaching
that a child learns how to do this. Joseph is a fine teacher of

emotional intelligence as are Mary and Kahlil. Obviously, Jesus is a truly gifted child, a genius in the domain of personal intelligence. His gifts are evident but they are enhanced, growing deeper and stronger through the guidance of his teachers, his emotional coaches. Joseph does not try to take away his unusual capacity for feelings although he worries about how Jesus can survive with such sensitivity. There are times that Joseph questions whether the world is too cruel for someone with such a capacity for feeling and compassion, yet he does not ever try to take it away. Teachers of gifted students often comment that they are not really putting something into such a child, they are only helping bring something out that is unique and beautiful. I once overheard an elderly Russian ballet teacher say, "The special ones are born with the dance inside, I just try to make a way for it to come out." Joseph is that kind of emotional coach. He is a loving and kind coach and has passed through many hard lessons to develop his own intrapersonal intelligence and master his own feelings.

Consider how important intrapersonal skills are for your child in coping with the world and in coping with themselves. As Joseph's story illustrates, being able to be smart about yourself and your inner life is key to life success.

Intrapersonal Intelligence Skills

The following list includes some basic intrapersonal capabilities. As a father you will coach your child to develop simple skills in these areas.

1. The ability to concentrate and pay attention.

2. The ability to relax.

3. The ability to cope with fear, pain and anxiety.

4. The ability to be aware of and draw upon your imagination, imagery and dreams.

5. The ability to use personal physiology to control your breath, pulse and heart rate.

6. The ability to identify, discriminate between, and use and enjoy one's own feelings.

Let us look closer at these intrapersonal basics to see why they are so important.

1. The ability to concentrate and to pay attention.

You have certainly been aware of how your child has developed attention skills. You have probably also become aware of how distractible your child can be. It is a time-honored trick for parents to distract a child from things you do not want them to touch or look at by suddenly feigning interest and excitement in something else and exclaiming, "Oh, wow! Look at this!" and sure enough, those little feet come running. As a child grows and develops, it is increasingly important for them to be able to sustain attention and concentration on a task. It is a crucial intrapersonal intelligence to be able to focus, not to be distracted from the task by our own internal thoughts and feelings, or outside distractions. Joseph takes time with Jesus to help him learn carpentry skills. He pays attention to Jesus for long periods of time and helps Jesus stay on task in order to teach him attention skills. He focuses with him and teaches him the skills of attending to details.

2. The ability to relax.

There is nothing so taken for granted as relaxing and just taking it easy. Yet, is it easy to just relax? Apparently not, if we look at the enormous amount of money spent on tranquilizers and chemical means of relaxing in our fast and stressful culture. We tend to accept adults having a tall cool one after a tough day, or thinking of Miller time or Valium time, but we fail to consider that, after a tough day of second grade, most children cannot simply circle twice like kittens and doze right off. Our children have high levels of stress. They have trouble sleeping and relaxing. Tense and nervous children are as common as tense and nervous adults. After all, where do you think all those tense and nervous adults come from? The ability to relax or to fall asleep consists of sets of skills. You can show your child how to systematically tense and release their muscles to promote relaxation. You can develop a ritual of reading them to sleep while teaching them skills to fall asleep.

3. The ability to cope with fear, pain and anxiety.

Fear, pain and anxiety are as common to life as joy, happiness and tranquility. Somehow we are taught to expect the latter and think there is something wrong with us if we are experiencing the former. Since we think it is bad to experience fear, pain or anxiety we learn to hide those feelings— generally with bad consequences. Those bottled-up feelings have nowhere to go. When we hide from them, we do not learn to handle them effectively. Joseph coaches Jesus through his fears, hurts, anxieties, and physical and emotional pain. Helping your own child to realize that fear, pain and anxiety are a part of life and teaching him or her how to identify and handle those feelings are great gifts to your child.

4. The ability to be aware of and draw upon imagination, imagery and dreams.

This is a rich developmental area for children that we, as adults, fail to recognize. Imagination is an essential component of creativity and, like a muscle, can get stronger with exercise or just atrophy away with disuse. Imagery can be a rich source of help in dealing with feelings and as a tool for health and healing. Children can become adept dreamers and, with parental encouragement and support, readily learn to become lucid dreamers with the awareness to help themselves deal with fears and other feeling problems while they sleep. Joseph's dreams were rich sources of personal and spiritual growth for him. During times of stress, he would go to his mountaintop to pray, meditate and dream. He tells us how Jesus helped the suffering slaves on the ship by taking them home through their imaginations with music and song.

5. The ability to control and use your personal physiology.

This may seem like an unusual aspect of intrapersonal intelligence for your child and yet it is an important one in terms of managing stress. How can control of bodily functions help us? Consider that biofeedback experts taught patients with irregular heart rhythms to normalize their heart patterns. Some people have been taught to regulate their blood flow to warm their hands and feet and to relax by regulating their brain rhythms with meditation or prayer. Sport psychologists help elite athletes control brain and body to enhance performance. While these are sophisticated examples, children can be easily taught skills that are the building blocks of these advanced techniques.

The "Lemon Exercise" is one of the first exercises taught to Division I athletes at Alabama A&M University. Try it with your child. Just say:

Let's exercise our imagination and see how our mind can make things happen in our body. Imagine that I am handing you a big fresh lemon. Imagine that it is bright yellow. Now bring that imaginary lemon to your nose and smell it. Now imagine that we are going to take a knife and slice that lemon in half. It is so juicy inside, and the juice is dripping off the lemon, so we bring it right to our mouth and lick that lemon with our tongue.

By now, your child may be reacting just as the athletes do. They pucker up and salivate. That lemony feeling is in their mouth, but where is the lemon? Their own imagination created that physiological change. The lesson is that what you think about changes how you feel. What if you think negative and scary thoughts? What if you think positive and strong thoughts about yourself? The same thing happens as with the lemon exercise. Imagine thinking of bright, sunny days. Then think of someone that loves you smiling at you, you smile back and then that person hugs you. You get the idea. You can easily coach your child in this simple exercise that can have profound effects physically and psychologically.

6. Identify, discriminate between, understand, use and enjoy one's own feelings.

This is the keystone of intrapersonal intelligence. To have access to this ability and to develop an increasing set of skills will mean that a child can live well with his or her own self. There seems to be nothing so terrible as the troubles we bring upon ourselves by not being able to deal with our own emotions and thoughts. There is no escape from ourselves except through the temporary oblivion of drugs or alcohol, or the extreme escape of suicide which, sadly, is an escalating choice of teens.

Stress-resilient children show an example of how feelings can work for you. Stress-resilient children are of special interest to many psychologists due to their unique ability to tolerate extreme amounts of stress and yet continue to thrive. These kinds of children have been found in Israeli border towns, in strife-torn Belfast, Ireland, and in extremely violent and depressed inner-city environments in the United States. All of the children identified as stress-resilient seem to have the extraordinary capability to not only tolerate the stress that debilitates others in the environment, but to maintain a high level of personal functioning. Interestingly enough the characteristics of these children are remarkably similar to children with especially high self-esteem. An important component of intrapersonal intelligence is the capability of using our feelings to work for us in difficult situations. This kind of capability can also allow children to have the capacity to take risks, try new tasks and therefore provide new opportunities for growth and learning.

It is no mystery, then, that those children who are not able to develop intrapersonal intelligence skills have only to turn to drugs and alcohol to escape their pain. It is our responsibility as parents to help our children to help themselves by coaching them in these skills and providing our own best skills as models. Joseph spent a great deal of time teaching and coaching Jesus about feelings. Remember that he worked with feelings almost as much as he taught carpentry skills to Jesus. Remember the removing of the splinter.

Interpersonal Intelligence

The other main subdivision of personal intelligence is called interpersonal intelligence. According to Gardner, this is: ". . . the ability to notice and make distinctions among other individuals and in particular, among their moods, temperaments, motivations and intentions. In an advanced form interpersonal knowledge permits a skilled adult to read the intentions and desires—even when these have been hidden—of many other individuals and, potentially, to act upon this knowledge, for example, by influencing a group of disparate individuals to behave along desired lines."[6] Simply stated, it is being smart about other people.

Stop and think for a minute about the genuinely likable and personally influential individuals that you have met in

6. Gardner, 239.

your life so far. Think about the way those individuals seemed so effective in relating to not just you but to all sorts of people. These people with especially developed interpersonal intelligence are the superior teachers, coaches, managers and leaders in our lives. Very often, they are capable of "reading" other people's potential and helping them to bring out the best in their abilities.

Every child needs to develop various sets of interpersonal skills. Ideally as the child grows older, increasingly sophisticated forms of interpersonal skills develop. The following are some basic interpersonal skills. There certainly are others, but these are basics that should be considered important for everyday success in school and life.

Interpersonal Intelligence Skills

1. The ability to love and to be loved, to make human contact. To be able to initiate, maintain and enrich human relationships.
2. The ability to work and play and to participate appropriately and skillfully with individuals and groups.
3. The ability to read and understand nonverbal communication.
4. The ability to communicate clearly and effectively with individuals and groups.
5. The ability to listen, understand and empathize with others.
6. The ability to encourage, motivate, direct and manage others in a manner that enhances their behaviors, attitudes and performance.

While you might not expect your child to grow up to be excellent in all of these interpersonal skills, not to have the basics in any one of these is a handicap. Let us look at each one briefly and see why they are so important to growing up successfully.

1. The ability to love and to be loved, to make human contact. To be able to initiate, maintain and enrich human relationships. This one is listed number one on purpose. This is the most important human ability. Without this ability we are condemned to a life of loneliness and aloneness, and the probability of our enjoying a successful and happy life is severely impacted. Being open to relationships, to be able to develop friendships and intimacy, is a key component to personal intelligence. A child experiences emotional pain from being cut off and isolated from others. Consider that the most effective and painful kind of human torture is isolation.

   All children at some level long to be liked—to be cared about—to have the positive regard of their peers. To be an "outsider"—to be outside of the positive regard of peers— can be agony. The eroding effect of being an outsider on a child's self-esteem cannot be overestimated. The following is the day-to-day experience of a school child.

CINDY

I was one of "the walking dead." Every day at school I walked numbly from class to class. I walked with my head down, never looking at anyone. No one ever looked at me anyway and it saved me having to feel worse by seeing groups of people with their friends. I had no one to sit by. It sounds dumb, but to go to lunch every day in the cafeteria and have no one to sit by, it was unbearable. To see other girls and boys laughing together with their "in" jokes and plans. It just hurt. How I got to be this way and they were the way they were, I just didn't know. I was dumb. I was really smart in math and everything else. It seemed like somehow everyone else had been told a secret and I hadn't. I didn't know how to make friends. I pretended I didn't care. Now I do know how. I know how to approach people and have the confidence to reach out, and care and show that I do. Sometimes I dream I am back there, and I am "the walking dead" again—it is my worst nightmare.

Children, without affirming relationships, fail to thrive. In spite of special gifts in other kinds of intelligence, a child without interpersonal intelligence skills will suffer. Without this core ability to relate, to develop relationships, to become close to another, and to love and be loved, any child's future is limited.

2. The ability to work and play and to participate appropriately and skillfully with individuals and groups.

A recent survey of top corporations revealed that the characteristic that top managers prized most was "employability." They said that far more than school grades or I.Q. test scores, the trait they look for most is the ability to work well with others. They reported that the trait that doomed talented people to failure most often was the inability to get along with people. Getting along with others. It sounds funny coming from big Fortune 500 companies, doesn't it? It sounds like something on your third grade report card. It probably was on your third grade report card. The problem is that the sets of skills that make up "getting along with others" are not taught in schools. Some children have these skills and many do not. For those who do, they have all the right moves. For those who do not, social situations are always difficult. It is here that your emotional coaching is essential. Getting along with others is a critical life success skill. A father who plays with his child is laying down the foundation for the future. Earlier we talked about the father who was playing at wrestling and fighting with his boys. Remember how he showed the boys how to be aggressive and yet play fair, and to become aware of their own strength and aggression. It is no accident that that father is the very successful president of his own company and a gifted manager of people. He is passing along those skills by playing with his boys. Joseph made a point of making this kind of play very important.

3. The ability to read and understand nonverbal communication.

Communication experts report that the importance of nonverbal communication is undeniable. Experts have noted that the words in a conversation carry less than 35 percent of the meaning of the situation. They note that nearly two-thirds of what we communicate is through body language. Children are remarkably responsive to nonverbal communication. In a well-known study, teachers were told at the beginning of the school year that certain students had done very well on a test of intellectual ability. Amazingly, or really not so amazingly, those students showed a sharp rise in their scores on an actual test at the end of the year. The conclusion of the researchers was that the students' responded to their teachers' nonverbal communication throughout the year by developing a new high regard for themselves as well as higher intellectual expectations. Obviously the opposite is also possible. Low regard and low expectations are always obvious to our children. Coaching about nonverbal communication is important. How your child moves and walks says a lot about them. Ask them about how the way someone walks reveals things about that person. What can they say about just the way someone looks? Are they proud, respectful, sad, feeling low?

4. The ability to communicate clearly and effectively with individuals and groups.

Personally intelligent people have developed the skills to speak effectively. In fact, there is probably nothing so obvious that sets personally intelligent people apart from others than being able to speak effectively. Nearly every day in national surveys a remarkable fact reoccurs. When adults are asked to name their top fears, the one that always tops the list is speaking to a group. To be able to speak effectively and communicate clearly is a set of skills that truly sets one apart from the norm. These are the people who become the leaders and managers. This does not mean that all of these people are extroverts. There are many shy people who have managed to develop the skills of effective speaking and communication. It is a matter of developing the ability, not changing how you are inside. Part of this can develop just from being listened to at the dinner table. Ask your children questions and respectfully listen to what they have to say. Hear their opinions and ideas. You will be helping them develop this special skill.

5. The ability to listen well and to respond to other people's deeper feelings—to have empathy.

To be able to listen well and be able to empathize with other people's feelings is one of the cornerstones of emotional intelligence. Entire courses are devoted to these sets of skills in the advanced training of counselors, psychologists, psychiatrists, nurses and doctors. Why devote so much time to the training of something that seems to be so basic as just listening when someone is talking? Because by the time we are adults we are doing it so poorly. In Joseph's story he is amazed by Jesus' ability to deeply understand other people. Jesus of course is representative of the highest possible ability in this realm. But, remember he tells Joseph that anyone could understand if they would just listen. You can listen to your child. Hear what they say. Pay attention with your heart as well as your ears. Your children will learn this from you, and they will be special in their relationships.

6. The ability to encourage, motivate, direct and manage others in a manner that enhances their behaviors, attitudes and performance.

Here we are talking about sets of interpersonal skills that benefit and bring out the best in others. One individual who illustrates these qualities and this kind of interpersonal intelligence is basketball coach John Wooden. The most successful coach in college basketball history, he was known as the "Wizard of Westwood" during his coaching days at UCLA. He had an uncanny ability to mold a disparate group of strong-willed, often spoiled and egotistical adolescents into a smoothly functioning team that was willing to sacrifice their individual glory for the good of the team. He did it year after year. Young players knew that he would be able to bring out the very best in their ability to play basketball.

I was able to observe Coach Wooden as a participant at a week-long camp for adults. Now, conducting a camp for middle-aged, portly and poorly talented basketball wannabes would seem to be a stunningly boring task for the greatest basketball coach in history, but not for John Wooden.

In his very first moments with you, the enthusiasm, drive and determination of his personality are apparent. In your first personal contact with him, you sincerely and genuinely feel he is deeply interested in you as a basketball player and a person. He puts everything about himself into being "your coach," and it is clear he is expecting no less in return. It is a deeply personal encounter with an absolutely genuine human being. Like other gifted teachers, coaches and managers, he has the interpersonal intelligence to make you almost immediately realize that he understands something about you that you had always been waiting and wanting someone to understand. He knows that you know that he knows—and that he is going to be able to bring out something inside you that he knows is there. In that moment you are suddenly more capable and confident.

I watched Coach Wooden do this with man after man. He put everything he had into every individual he worked with, and I am certain that he gave to each of us no less than to any of his All-Americans and Hall of Famers. That is his gift and he passes it on to everyone he coaches. I was changed in some way by just having the experience of being with him. That is the gift of those who are geniuses in this way. They are the great teachers and healers. Mother Teresa once was asked by a journalist, who was totally overwhelmed by the suffering and poverty surrounding him, how she could go on when it was so obvious that she couldn't help all the suffering people. She said that she wasn't helping all the people, she was only helping the one that was in front of her at that moment, and she was giving that one person everything that she had.

As a father you are doing just that. Trying to give all that you have to that one child you have in front of you. The consequences of your doing so are enormous. You will have done the emotional coaching that results in a personally intelligent child. Think of Joseph and all that he put into raising Jesus. He put his whole life and his whole heart into raising him. Our children deserve no less.

The Final Tractate of the Blue Codice

I was at the harbor and had finished arranging passage when Kahlil and Jesus found me. "We have been looking for you, old friend," Kahlil said. "I know what is in your heart."

"We want you to go with us, Father," said Jesus.

"I cannot, I must leave and do this," I said.

"Come with us, spend just this day and this night with us," they both said. "If you still want to leave, then choose."

The Return to Nazareth

They had packed for traveling. I was mostly silent on this journey. I was not paying much attention and was surprised when I found that we were at the place by the sea where I had always taken the children for our special time. Kahlil's uncle had brought James, Mary and Esther.

We sat by the fire with the stars above us, and Jesus told a story about John. He laughed and he cried as he told of his little brother and the first time that he caught a fish. Kahlil recalled when John took the silk rug from his library to give to the beggar who had no legs. James told of when John saved a small dog from drowning at the harbor. Mary took my hand and said that she knew my heart was burning for revenge, traditional honor and respect, but that we two had gone our own way before and this seemed another time to go another way. "Here are all who love and respect you. If you go away and do this thing, then will not someone else come with their heart burning like yours and then want to kill you or James or Jesus?"

Kahlil said to me, "Old friend, honor the memory of your son not with blood."

Jesus took my hand, "Father, we need you. Do not go do this thing, for it will not heal your heart, give you more honor or bring you respect. Listen now to the voices of all that love you, not the voice of revenge. Can you hear us?" He reached out to me and touched my chest over my heart. "Can you hear the voice of our God, my Father?"

I tell you now, his hand then became hot like a fire, and I could feel the heat through my robe, and then on my skin and down to my own heart. In my own ears I heard, and this is true, the voice of my dead son John. "I love you, Father, and am with you always."

My own sorrow came, and I wept without shame for my little boy. That night God's angel came and spoke to me again.

The Third Great Dream

I was on a ship far from home.
Mary and all of our family were with me.
The sea rose in a great storm.
Winds, great bolts of lightning and claps of thunder.
I again had my knife.
I wanted revenge.
I searched and searched for my uncle and could not find him.
I was lost. The knife turned into a serpent that bit me again and again.

Then again the light from the sky and the clouds cleared and the Angel appeared.

"Go home now, Joseph, back to Nazareth."

Go home and raise Jesus. You have no need for blood. God has blessed you with his son. Go now to Galilee."

I saw the Angel ascend into the sky. Then I was standing on the prow of the ship with Jesus' hand in mine and Mary by my side. Ahead I saw my homeland.

In the morning, I rose early, and Jesus was sitting by me. We went to our place of prayers and prayed together.

"I am leaving, Father," he said. I turned to him. "I will return to our land with you for a little while and then I will leave. We can go back now because they all believe I am dead. Herod has died. Your uncle is old, and he thinks I am dead and believes his blood-thirst is satisfied. I will go home with you and then visit the great temple in Jerusalem. I do not want any more of my family to die for me. I will go home with you and then I will leave on a ship to begin my work." He embraced me then. I could feel in the muscles in his back, the sound of his voice and the strength in his heart that he was becoming a young man.

We sat together then, his hand in mine, as when he was a little boy watching the sunrise.

Moral/Spiritual Intelligence

There is another kind of intelligence embodied throughout Joseph's story, and that is what the gifted writer Robert Coles calls moral intelligence and what I will refer to as moral/spiritual intelligence.

Coles says that it is not something that is simply acquired. He says: "We grow morally as a consequence of learning how to be with others, how to behave in this world—a learning prompted by taking to heart what we have seen and heard. The child is a witness; the child is an ever-attentive witness of grown-up morality—or lack thereof; the child looks and looks for cues as to how one ought to behave, and finds them galore as we parents and teachers go about our lives, making choices, addressing people, show in action our rock-bottom assumptions, desires and values, and thereby telling those young observers much more than we realize."[7]

Throughout the story of Joseph, his deep spiritual connectedness to life, to nature and to his God is evident. His prayers and meditations are as natural a part of his daily life as working and eating. His moral and spiritual life are an everyday and essential part of his life.

Joseph is not a perfect man. He is us. He is human, flawed, immature, impetuous and self-righteous. He is also passionate, loving, weak, angry, stupid, fearful, hard-working and courageous. He is a great friend, family man, a loving husband, and a loving and kind father. When times are tough he turns to his prayers, meditations and his

---

7. Robert Coles, *The Moral Intelligence of Children* (New York: Random House, 1997), 5.

dreams. His inner life is important. He seeks awareness. He grows. He struggles throughout his story on his own soul road. He attains character and strongly, consciously and purposely develops his own moral/spiritual intelligence. He shows his children this way of living in the world and guides them toward the development of their own moral and spiritual intelligence.

The Good Enough Father

English pediatrician and child psychoanalyst D. W. Winnicott developed the concept of the "good enough mother." Let us take that concept for ourselves in being the "good enough father." This is not measured by our salaries or bank accounts or how many children we have. No, it is measured, he says, "by a daily life that gets affirmed by a particular child."[8] The daily actions with a child that are "sufficiently kind and thoughtful and sensitive, sufficiently present to the baby, at pains through thick and thin to nurture and protect and assist . . . the coaching by day and night."[9]

Coles says that coaching is a complex matter, and we know that by now from our reading of Joseph. We know that to be the "good enough father" we have to be fair and gentle and yet hard and tough enough to set the boundaries and be the protector and the guardians of our children. We have to love them enough to sometimes not be liked. We are sometimes the standards and the rules that are pushed on and challenged. We are also the standard of good. We must strive to be the father who

8. Coles, 92.
9. Coles, 92.

shows the good, expects the good and consequently raises the standard of goodness by being the "good enough father."

The Child Is the Father to the Man

Joseph has shown us the way toward being the good father in his story. Of course, he is raising the child who is becoming the personification of goodness. It is a mark of his good fathering that he has the awareness to allow and encourage Jesus to develop everything he can of his unique nature even when he clearly goes beyond Joseph's own understanding. The incident in the ship with the galley slaves is a good illustration. Joseph is able to stand aside and encourage Jesus' special gifts to shine and then is able to step forward and be the good father and emotional coach in nurturing and comforting Jesus in his pain.

Joseph's good fathering, like your good fathering, results in a child of goodness who grows into a good adult. If we could add up all of the aspects of the personal, moral and spiritual intelligence, then Jesus would embody the whole. This whole is far more than the parts. It is sacred. Jesus embodies for all of us what every child is to every father. A sacred gift to us allowing us to travel on our road of the soul. In following that road we will find that truly the child is father of the man.

There is more to Joseph's story, but we end it here for now. Remember that Joseph was only a man who was given something precious and sacred. Joseph grew into being a good father and so will you. Follow his lessons well, and Joseph will guide you along your own soul road in becoming a father.

I am old. I cannot see to write.

It is a dark night with many stars.

There is wind off the sea, and I am sleepy.

I can hear Mary and the children from far away.

Sometimes I cannot tell whether all of this was a part of one of my great dreams or not, but that is as it happened. End of Codice 1.

[Translator's note: The Blue Codice ends here.]

The story of our family's return to Nazareth, Jesus' visit to the temple in Jerusalem, and his disappearance and journey is in the red-bound codice.

[Translator's note: It appears that this last sentence was added by Joseph sometime after he finished the first Codice. The Red Codice is in translation].

READER/CUSTOMER CARE SURVEY

If you are enjoying this book, please help us serve you better and meet your changing needs by taking a few minutes to complete this survey. Please fold it & drop it in the mail.

As a special **"Thank You"** we'll send you news about interesting books and a valuable **Gift Certificate**.

PLEASE PRINT

NAME:_____

ADDRESS: _____

_____

TELEPHONE NUMBER: _____

FAX NUMBER: _____

E-MAIL: _____

WEBSITE: _____

(1) Gender: 1)_____Female 2)_____Male

(2) Age:

1)_____	12 or under	5)_____	30-39
2)_____	13-15	6)_____	40-49
3)_____	16-19	7)_____	50-59
4)_____	20-29	8)_____	60+

(3) Your Children's Age(s):

Check all that apply.

1)_____	6 or Under	3)_____	11-14
2)_____	7-10	4)_____	15-18

(7) Marital Status:

1)_____Married
2)_____Single
3)_____Divorced/Wid.

(8) Was this book

1)_____Purchased for yourself?
2)_____Received as a gift?

(9) How many Chicken Soup books have you bought or read?

1)_____	1	3)_____	3
2)_____	2	4)_____	4+

(10) How did you find out about this book?

Please check ONE.

1)_____Personal Recommendation
2)_____Store Display
3)_____TV/Radio Program
4)_____Bestseller List
5)_____Website
6)_____Advertisement/Article or Book Review
7)_____Catalog or mailing
8)_____Other_____

(11) What FIVE subject areas do you enjoy reading about most?

Rank: 1 (favorite) through 5 (least favorite)

A)_____ Self Development
B)_____ New Age/Alternative Healing
C)_____ Storytelling
D)_____ Spirituality/Inspiration
E)_____ Family and Relationships
F)_____ Health and Nutrition
G)_____ Recovery
H)_____ Business/Professional
I) _____ Entertainment
J) _____ Teen Issues
K)_____ Pets

(16) Where do you purchase most of your books?

Check the top TWO locations.

A)_____ General Bookstore
B)_____ Religious Bookstore
C)_____ Warehouse/Price Club
D)_____ Discount or Other Retail Store
E)_____ Website
F)_____ Book Club/Mail Order

(18) Did you enjoy the stories in this book?

1)_____Almost All
2)_____Few
3)_____Some

(19) What type of magazine do you SUBSCRIBE to?

Check up to FIVE subscription categories.

A)_____ General Inspiration
B)_____ Religious/Devotional
C)_____ Business/Professional
D)_____ World News/Current Events
E)_____ Entertainment
F)_____ Homemaking, Cooking, Crafts
G)_____ Women's Issues
H)_____ Other (please specify) _____

(24) Please indicate your income level

1)_____Student/Retired-fixed income
2)_____Under $25,000
3)_____$25,000-$50,000
4)_____$50,001-$75,000
5)_____$75,001-$100,000
6)_____Over $100,000

Additional comments you would like to make:

(31) Are you:

1) A Parent? _____

2) A Grandparent? _____

5) _____ Family/Relationship issues

4) _____ Job-related

3) _____ Religious/Spiritual

2) _____ Motivational

1) _____ Business/Financial

Check all that apply.

(26) If you answered yes, what type?

(25) Do you attend seminars?

(1) _____ Yes   (2) _____ No

Thank You!!

HCI

The Life Issues Publisher

FOLD HERE

BUSINESS REPLY MAIL

FIRST-CLASS MAIL PERMIT NO 45 DEERFIELD BEACH, FL

POSTAGE WILL BE PAID BY ADDRESSEE

HEALTH COMMUNICATIONS, INC.
3201 SW 15TH STREET
DEERFIELD BEACH, FL 33442-9875

**NO POSTAGE
NECESSARY
IF MAILED
IN THE
UNITED STATES**

PART II

STORIES OF FATHERHOOD

Introduction

This part contains stories written *by* fathers and stories written *about* fathers. We've all read about fathers who were never there and about fathers that should not have been there. This collection is different; it is a celebration of the fathers we wish we had and the ones we can strive to emulate.

These stories are about fathers who made a positive difference in their children's lives. These are fathers who are the modern-day equivalent to the biblical Joseph: men who were there for their children, sacrificed for them, loved and cared and nurtured them. The stories are not about perfect men being perfect fathers. They are about men going about the difficult and demanding work of fathering the best way they know how.

GROWING HEART AND SOUL

My father's parents emigrated from Lebanon in 1895. They found each other on this side of the sea, and began a life farming a homestead in North Dakota and raising eight children, four sons followed by four daughters. My father was the youngest son. The oldest son inherited the land in the old-country custom. When my father and his brother John returned from World War II, they started a small grocery business, and then moved to Cando, North Dakota, a town of fifteen hundred on the prairie, to form Nicholas Bros. Meat Processing and Sales. Farmers dropped off their livestock and came back later for neatly wrapped parcels of meat cut just the way they wanted it (Bill and John remembered each family's order after the first time).

My father met his bride, a teacher in a one-room schoolhouse, when he was forty-five. Theirs was a love that would last. They raised my sister and me in that little town, and there we learned all that was ever important. My father's lessons formed my heart and soul.

He taught me the value of home and family. For recreation, we planted trees, flowers and a garden around our little house, which was right next to Nicholas Bros. Meat Processing and Sales. We puttered around in a little duck boat in the pond out back. A favorite outing was when the four of us would ride out to Snyder Lake with a picnic of salami on crackers, and watch Lady, our Labrador retriever, fetch sticks that Daddy threw in the water. A favorite excursion was to drive around town on a summer evening and then go out to Dairy Land for an ice cream cone dipped in chocolate. On other family outings we would drive around looking at Christmas lights or go to the fairgrounds to watch fireworks on the Fourth of July.

My father taught me to honor and appreciate my country. He was a Legionnaire and always carried the colors in parades on Memorial Day and Veterans Day. I was a member of the American Legion Junior Auxiliary because of his influence. I still feel American pride and get a lump in my throat when I hear "The Star Spangled Banner" or "America the Beautiful."

Another lifelong lesson my father taught me was the importance of helping those less fortunate, and seeing the good in everyone. This took the form of sharing our hearts. We didn't have much money, but Daddy always had a way of reaching out to the people in town who were rejected by others. Elmer Cook was one example. He was "slow," and had an odd way of walking and talking. He mostly walked around with his head down looking sad, but when he came to Nicholas Bros. he would laugh and joke within minutes. When we saw him uptown, Daddy would include him like any other friend. Nobody would have thought of making a disparaging remark about Elmer around my father.

I grew up spending most of my time at the meat plant so I could be near my dad. The pleasures of friendship and camaraderie punctuated the days. At 10 A.M., a group of businessmen from uptown would come to the plant for coffee. They would roll dice and bet nickels and dimes, laugh, and talk politics and business. My father would grind up fresh beef, and they would eat it raw on crackers with salt and pepper. Another group would come for their afternoon coffee and the same lighthearted break. Dad's chuckle was the heartiest of all.

I learned about working hard and saving money by watching my father. I have a letter he sent to his mother during the war when he was in Guam, in which he wrote about missing his family. He told them he had bought them a fifty-dollar bond, and would get another one when he got paid. I still have the bankbook he kept for me when I was growing up, and it is touching to see how he faithfully stashed away (ten dollars at a time) a nest egg for my college education. He worked hard all week, and I remember him whistling or humming a tune while he worked. He always seemed to have a Band-Aid on one finger or another where the knife had slipped while he cut steaks and chops. His nails were neatly trimmed, and the skin on his hands was smooth and firm from working in the tallow all day. He taught me to cut and wrap the meat just so, and was patient with me as I developed coordination.

He shared his favorite hobby, too. He was a rifleman who loved hunting and shooting at the club. He led the "Dakota Junior Rifle Club," which meant he taught my friends and me about gallery shooting and drove us throughout the state for competitions. He would cheer us all on, and I was proud that all the other kids thought he was as cool as I did.

Daddy, Uncle John and I would go gopher hunting on the weekends. The farmers were glad for us to shoot the pesky prairie dogs, and we had a grand time doing it. I remember how he would help me aim, and show me how to squeeze the trigger ever so gently.

My sister and I always knew we were beautiful to our dad. At Easter, he would go to the Style Shop, bring us home hats and dresses and then tell us how pretty we looked in them. I felt like a princess.

He and Mom taught us about romantic love, too, without trying. Mom would make Syrian flatbread some mornings, and we would wait by the door for Daddy to come home for lunch because we knew he would kiss her, and we would giggle and they would laugh at our giggling. When they got ready to go out on Saturday nights, Mom would put on a nice dress and fix her hair fancy. I could tell he thought she was the most beautiful woman in the world, and she would glow looking at him. It was customary to dance with everyone at the local dances. I heard Dad tell Mom many times that he was so relieved when he finished dancing with the other women and could get back to her, because it was like gliding around the floor, she was so smooth.

Connie Nicholas Carnes

BRAIDING HAIR

I was having a hard time going through a divorce. I was emotionally strung out. On the outside I apparently looked okay, but I knew I was just hanging on day-by-day. My daughter was six years old. I felt terrible, but I felt even more terrible for her. She was doing all the work that kids do in that kind of situation. She'd be extra good and try like hell to get her mom and dad back on track. It was hard for her to hold all her emotions together but she tried. She tried especially hard during her stays at "Dad's house."

I felt as though I had always had a close relationship with her, but I really had not been all that responsible for her. I had diapered, bathed, fed and played with her, but always as the backup caretaker. Now it was different. I had her with me at my house, I was it, and there was no backup for me. It is hard to overestimate how difficult it all seemed then. It was difficult in part because I had yet to make a real commitment to really caring for her. It all came out on a Monday morning.

It was time to get ready for school. We had to eat something. I had to call the office. I had to be in L.A. for an appointment. She had to get dressed. She was tired. We had come back late from the beach and she was sunburned. I had to get dressed. I had to check the answering service. There were all these things to do, and we were running out of time. Then she came to me with a brush and a rubber band and said, "Daddy, you have to braid my hair."

I said, "I can't braid your hair, Kelly. I don't know how."

"You have to, Daddy, you have to, I can't go to school without my hair braided."

It is hard even now to describe that moment. It was as if everything that was wrong and everything I was doing wrong was coming together around not being able to braid her hair. There seemed to be a frantic tension between us. She needed me to do this. I did not know how. I did not have time for this. I had an office to get to. I had an appointment waiting in L.A. I had an hour-and-a-half drive ahead of me just to get there. She had to get to school. The clock was ticking. "We cannot do this, Kelly," I said again. "I do not have time and I do not know how." She started to cry.

"You have to!" she said, crying louder.

"I do not have to," I said. "I have to get to work!"

"You are supposed to take care of me!" she said, crying louder now and sobbing.

"I am taking care of you!"

"Mommy braids my hair," she was sobbing louder.

"I am not Mommy and I have to get to work!"

"You don't care about me."

"I do, too, and you know it, and we have to get going right now!"

And then I stopped. I remember choosing something right then. I felt like just picking her up, carrying her out to the car and driving her to school—and that would be that.

I looked down at her. She was crying and she was giving in—not really—she was giving up. She was giving up on me taking care of her.

She was right. I wasn't taking care of her, really. I was still taking care of myself. I was going to put me first here. My job was important, my appointment was important, my time was important. She wasn't that important. Okay.

I sat down in the chair. I was so frustrated and wound-up I was ready to cry, or break things or, easiest of all, just yell at her, pick her up and physically make her do what I wanted.

I decided.

I decided to care for her. I decided to care for her first. I decided to be her father for as much as it took. I had had my way all my life. I had better grow up and be a father.

"I don't know how to do this, Kelly," I said. "You'll have to tell me how to braid your hair. Just sit down here and hold the mirror and we'll do this together." I began to brush her hair. I took a deep breath. I was very awkward. It was hard to hold her hair in the three strands and then cross them over. My hands felt too big and too clumsy. I did it wrong. I had to start over again. This wasn't a guy thing. No! For sure this *was* a father thing. I think that we both had tears running down our face, but she was smiling and I was being her Daddy. I learned how to make "not very good braids" that morning. I rearranged my appointment. We got to school a little late. We walked up the path to her classroom together. I remember holding her hand, and her hair looked really pretty in the sunlight even though the braid was a little crooked and messy. I had started learning how to be her father.

John L. Hart

FATHERING MILLIE

I met Milandra when she was a little over two years old. I waited in the car as Jaymie, her mother, went to retrieve her from daycare. I can still remember the toddling blond little girl proudly pushing open a side gate and approaching the car. I gave her a big smile. When she saw me, she cried. Jaymie comforted her, and soon enough we pushed her around town in her stroller. We visited shops, played with toys, read children's books, had a few drinks (orange juice, sodas) and called it a night around 8:30. When my dates climbed into their station wagon, Millie waved good-bye and gave me a smile—her large, beautiful hazel eyes shining.

It's four years later, and Millie is down the street making Easter baskets with her mother and two younger brothers: Isaac, two and a half; and Holden, three months. My first experience with fatherhood was not a biological one; while the depths of unconditional love for my sons was instinctual, fathering Millie has been and continues to be a rich and challenging lesson in honesty and the meaning of fatherhood.

I remember when she started calling me Dad. In her wisdom she wanted to wait until after Jaymie and I were married, though we had been together a couple of years and were living in a small, one-bedroom guesthouse. I was discovering a lot of wonderful things about raising a child, about being a family, and how soothing it can be to push a two-year-old on a swing. I was discovering how a child can make the sudden rush of a hummingbird's passing a memorable and explosive moment; how, sitting together under our covered porch and watching a torrential downpour, memories of my own childhood were reawakened.

But I was also struggling. As Millie's father figure, I was in a land of unexplored and undefined territory. Taking her out for ice cream was easy, but what if she won't brush her teeth before bed? Jaymie and I agreed that I would assume all paterntal duties. Yet I was still uncomfortable, just as Jaymie had difficulty letting go of even a part of parenting the daughter she had raised with so much devotion.

So I thought happily of the day she would call me Dad. The label, I was convinced, would cement our bond. We would marry, my adoption of Millie would go through, and the confusion would disappear. Yet when it happened, when she dropped "Gabriel" for "Daddy," I felt very awkward. It wasn't quite me she was talking to.

I was doing everything right! I adopted her, I took her to school, gave her baths, read her bedtime stories. My family had not only accepted her, but also showered her with attention and love. There was no biological father in the picture. And yet I was feeling pressure, resentment and a host of other "ugly" feelings: *Here is someone who is not my blood calling me Dad. She isn't my kid!* My romantic conception, my image of "Daddy," was being violated. For someone who considers himself a pretty good guy, this was the heart of darkness. Where did these feelings come from? Was it the working of evolution? Was my image of fatherhood being destroyed by an instinctual impulse to care only for my own genes?

And on top of that there was the public eye. I didn't like the term "stepdaughter." She has my last name—she's mine. I became embarrassed and uneasy when people asked about her birth or commented on whom she looked like. A wide range of jealousies spooked my dreams. My ego was constantly bruised. I wasn't feeling particularly like "Dad" at the time. I was confused.

This confusion lasted until the birth of my first son, Isaac.

Here it was. Here were the biological stirrings, the unconditional love and intense bliss of fatherhood. Being a father, I discovered right away, was not an act of will. There was never a breaking point where I *decided* to be Isaac's father or feel such a depth of love. There was no image of fatherhood here. I was giving more of myself than I ever thought possible, and loving it.

So Isaac's coming gave me perspective and helped me see that there was no cellular map to raising Millie. It released lots of the pressure I was putting on myself to be the perfect dad to Millie, to prove that she belonged to me, to fit her into my image of family, to protect my ego. All this stuff about "Dad" was in fact eclipsing the real love I felt for my little companion, which continues to deepen.

I couldn't will myself to be a father to Millie. And that was exactly what I had been doing. Our relationship is intrinsically different than Isaac's and mine, or Jaymie and hers. I am her adopted father. She feels a difference, too. And this difference isn't bad; it's just true. Ironically, for all my striving, acknowledging this difference has freed me to be a better father and friend to her. We are growing a relationship like any other human beings, with the extraordinary circumstance that we have become father and daughter. Since I've been able to let go of my image and deconstruct "Daddy," I can honestly say that becoming a father is not limited to blood relations. To my surprise, I'm relaxed about her upbringing.

When people ask, I tell them the truth. "She looks like her mom, but she has her biological father's eyes."

Tonight Millie and I read *The Giant's Foe* while Jaymie sang to Isaac and Holden lay asleep in her arms. I tucked my daughter into bed, wished her sweet dreams, gave her a kiss and told her I loved her.

Gabriel Arquilevich

MY FATHER

I recall my first experience accompanying my father to work, when I was ten years old. Holding his strong arms and skipping along trying to keep up with his big strides was awesome. I was so proud. His six-foot, two-inch frame fitted handsomely in his well-starched khaki uniform and his spit-shined size thirteen boots. This was the dress of a psychiatric nurse aide at Kingston's Bellevue Hospital, known throughout the island as "The Mad House." My father provided physical custody and rudimentary care for adults suffering from an array of mental, emotional and psychological problems.

It was the first of several trips I would make because I was totally fascinated with his work and spent considerable time wondering about mental illness and its causes, and why the experts could not find a cure for it. I thought that one day I would like to work in this field. This was the late 1940s and early 1950s, and psychotropic medications had not yet been discovered; mental illness was still a mysterious, supernatural phenomenon against which the public should be protected. No wonder these poor souls were locked away in a huge institution surrounded by a guarded perimeter fence. Treatment was harsh and cruel, especially if the workers thought that the patient was aware of their behavior.

I never understood why this warehouse of a prison was called a hospital. My father would apologize to the patients for using brute force to restrain and gain compliance, and told them that it was necessary for their own good and for the good of everyone around them. "There must be a better way to take care of these poor people," I said to my Dad. "Well, my son, these people are mad and don't feel or understand the same as you and I or normal people do. They are a lot better off in here than back in their homes, on the streets or in the countryside where people are deathly afraid of them and will treat them like wild animals to be hunted and even killed."

I understood, but still believed the whole thing unfair.

My father was the best at his job. He took it seriously and never missed a day if he could help it. He earned the respect and admiration of his coworkers and supervisors alike. Similarly, he was the most popular person in our neighbor-hood, and everyone knew that they could turn to Mr. Henry in good times or bad.

Born and raised in a small village in the Parish of Clarendon, Jamaica, British West Indies, my father, William Henry, was sent to the big city of Kingston at thir-teen to live with relatives where the opportunity for educa-tion was greater than in his village. After completing elementary school at fourteen, my father dropped out of school because there was no money for him to attend high school. Unlike America, high school in Jamaica was not free but an expensive and scarce commodity available to those who could afford it and who resided in certain areas. He studied auto mechanics and became a chauffeur for a manufacturing company. The work was not steady and with a wife and three children he began looking for more permanent work. On a fluke he applied for a job at the mental hospital, which was seeking young, strong men with kind hearts and an ability to learn. He landed the job and although the salary was not "wonderful," as he would say, it was a secure government job with the status of civil servant. He was twenty-two, and his new job was as a psychiatric aide at Kingston's Bellevue Hospital where he provided care for persons suffering a range of short-, medium- and long-term psychiatric illnesses. This job became his lifelong profession. After thirty years of dedicated service, he retired prematurely because of an automobile accident that left him disabled. He was seen by all as an industrious man, and when not at work he would undertake various projects at home involving all the children who were able to help. We quickly learned that once you enlisted or were designated for a project, you had no choice in the matter.

My father raised ten children; eight were his natural children, and two belonged to his wife from a previous relationship. He and my mother committed themselves to raising these children in a traditional home where my mother was the stay-at-home housewife with the kind and gentle touch, and my father the breadwinner and strong disciplinarian who commanded respect at all times, even when he was not physically present. Just the mention of his name, "Wait until your father gets home," would strike psychological fear. Whenever I think of my father, I think of the words, strong, hard-working, disciplinarian, courageous, dependable, kind, considerate and God-fearing. In retrospect, he was my role model, my hero.

The greatest legacy of my father—not only to me, but also to all of his children—was the intense desire for a good education. Although he was not educated, he knew that the only way to succeed in the British colony of Jamaica was through higher education. In fact, he said, "You children will have an education, even if I have to sell the very shirt off my back." My father knew that education for the indigenous population was not a priority for the colonial government. Hence, for the poor of Jamaica, education was a scarce resource and only the very best students were given the opportunity to compete for limited spots in the few secondary schools that existed. Once a student was admitted into a secondary school, they had to demonstrate ongoing excellence through hard work and keen competition to remain there because other students were literally standing in line for your spot. The concept of "social promotion" did not exist.

Consequently, my father sacrificed, struggled, borrowed, begged and did everything legally possible so that his children could go on to high school and, after high school, college. My father provided both incentives and disincentives for education. For example, we would be given a monetary reward for being among those students with the highest grade-point average. Similarly, we would be given accolades at home, including a special meal. With respect to disincentives, we would be permitted to observe a highway work crew using pickaxes and shovels to dig ditches in ninety-degree temperatures; or prisoners breaking rocks with sledgehammers in hot, dusty quarries; or sugarcane workers using machetes in the noon sun. We also witnessed a barefoot young man dressed in rags and pushing a hand-cart laden with agriculture products for the entrepreneurial street vendor. Then, my father would ask, in one of his no-nonsense voices, if these were the kinds of jobs we would like to do when we became adults and for the rest of our lives. It was quite sobering.

I truly did not know the extent of the impact of his influence on my life until I was alone, away from home, on a college campus in the United States learning to cope with a new culture and new beginnings. It was then that I realized that the values my parents and home had inculcated in me served me well. I could compete effectively with students from other countries and the United States. I could socialize effectively. I had a great sense of self-esteem and pride in who I was and in the work I did, all because of my identity with my strong father. I was not afraid to compete with anyone and to stand toe-to-toe, eye-to-eye and shoulder-to-shoulder regardless of race, socioeconomic status, gender or any other characteristics that tend to differentiate human beings. After receiving a bachelor's degree in economics and sociology, I suddenly realized that I wanted to be a psychiatric social worker. Like my father, I wanted to provide the best care possible for mentally ill patients and their families, and to help shape and influence public mental-health policy. Incidentally, a part of my training for my Master of Social Work degree was done at a state psychiatric hospital in Oregon.

As I became a man, a husband and father of two children, and a mental-health professional, I began to realize the enormity of the task my father had before him as he accepted the responsibility for his wife and ten children. In a poor country, how would he provide for their physical, mental, psychological, educational, social, moral and spiritual needs and development? It must have been totally overwhelming. As I faced my own challenges as a father, I constantly asked myself, "How did he do it?" Needless to say, his life became an increasing inspiration to me.

His dream for his children came true as he watched most of them graduate from college and become important citizens, not only in Jamaica, but also in America and Europe. One of the proudest moments my father and I shared was when I became a mental-health consultant to the director of the psychiatric hospital in Kingston from which my father retired. It was a great victory to him that one of his children could have gained a Ph.D. degree in a mental-health profession and returned to the island to be a consultant to his former top boss. He was proud to tell former coworkers and friends that I was his son. It was a time of celebration and reminiscing about the "good old days."

When my father became ill in 1980, two years after the death of my mother, I instinctively knew that I had to return to Jamaica to be with him. Even though it was a great sacrifice, my family supported the decision to return to Jamaica and spend time with him in appreciation for the life he had lived and the manner in which he had supported his family. After eighteen months, his health improved significantly, and we returned to America. My siblings and I encouraged him to spend time here or in England, but he thought that he was too old to travel and did not believe that it was possible for humans to fly. My family and I have never regretted the time spent with him. He lived another five years. Upon his death, I returned to Jamaica and gave the eulogy on behalf of my nine siblings, and his thirty grandchildren and eight great-grandchildren. He died a very happy and contented man. In many ways, he lives on in me today.

Mel Henry

THE SHIPYARD

My father died when he was sixty years old. He was a strong man and he worked on the docks at the shipyards until bone cancer broke him.

I always remember him dressed in a pressed blue work shirt, black jeans and big brown work boots. A pair of leather gloves would be in his back pocket, and he carried a big black metal lunch pail. I would sit on the grass in the front yard looking for his truck to come up the hill at the end of the day. He would get out of his old Ford pickup after a day in the shipyards smelling of the grease and oil and grime of ships from far away. He would pick me up and say, "How's my John-a-boy?" Then I would take his lunch pail and he would take my hand and we would walk around to the back porch and into dinner.

I remember the strength in his hands and arms and how hard he worked all year—usually twelve- and fourteen-hour days, six and seven days a week. Most of all I remember a day in the shipyards when I was fifteen. It was the first week of my first year working in the shipyard and it was rough on the docks. The work was rough and hard and so were many of the men who worked there. I did not know yet how to do the work of a rigger: tying off the lines of huge tankers and freighter ships, signaling the crane operators to life, and moving and gently lowering the enormous loads from the dock to the ships.

One man in the crew seemed to take a particular disliking to me being there. Hal was a big, beefy red-faced man with a bellowing voice and hard looks who seemed to take pleasure in belittling me by yelling about my mistakes and slowness and my general ineptitude.

It was finally Friday and late in the day: a blustery December day with gusty winds and icy rain. Hal told me to go on board and load a plate of steel. It was a tricky and difficult job because of the wind, and he should have done it. I wasn't supposed to load—just hook on and signal from the dock. He was giving the orders and made sure I knew it. He had me running back and forth doing both jobs, and he enjoyed yelling at my slow and fumbling efforts as I learned how to handle the hook on the crane and signal the loads up, away, and back down.

As I stood on board the ship waiting, a big sheet of steel plate weighing at least one ton came swinging toward me. Not experienced enough to know what I was doing, I signaled the load to swing toward me, and I backed up toward the ship. The wind caught the plate like a sail, and I found myself against the wall of the ship with two thousand pounds of steel sailing toward my chest. Someone yelled, and the crane operator's face was a frozen silent shout.

I dropped and rolled as the sound of the impact of the steel against the ship boomed out across the entire shipyard. The deck exploded in noise and shook beneath me as the load dropped just a few inches from where I had been standing. I was shaking and could barely breathe. Whistles and a siren sounded from the crane. He had activated the alarms thinking I had been crushed under the plate.

I jumped up and walked down the gangway to the dock. Hal was running and screaming and cursing at me, and threatening to throw me in the river. Behind him I saw my father running with the rest of the crew. The rage on his face was terrible. I was certain I was fired or worse. I had embarrassed him in front of his men, and I thought he was going to whip me right there. But the rage was not for me.

He grabbed Hal by the shirt and shook him. "You are supposed to be on that ship—not the boy!" he roared. Voices of assent arose from the crew.

"You want to work here, you'll do your job. You'll tell him you're sorry. You will treat him like any other man here."

There was a tense pause and Hal extended his hand. "Sorry. I was wrong. Sorry," he said.

As we walked off the dock, my dad put his arm around my shoulder. There were tears running down his cheeks.

The last summer of his life, we were on our way to the stadium for a ball game. It was a warm evening and the sun was setting, turning the sky purple and red. We started to cross the street and he grabbed my hand as he stepped off the curb. He held onto it as we walked toward the stadium and continued to walk hand-in-hand down the steps to our seats. He let me buy the peanuts and beer that time. I will never forget my dad.

John L. Hart

WORKING WITH LOVE

I remember riding to school in my father's pick-up truck, the dashboard covered with an odd assortment of screws and nails. With every turn and bump the entire truck rattled like a hardware store in an earthquake. Behind the seats in the cab were rolls of yellowed plans from houses and room additions he had built over the years. And in the bed of the truck was an even greater potpourri of spilled nails and miscellaneous hardware mixed in with scraps of lumber, plywood and dry-wall. Behind his seat were leftovers from the same houses and additions on the old plans. As he drove me to school and himself to work, he would listen to morning talk-radio and laugh and comment on the topic of the day. One morning, with the glower of an adolescent, I grumbled, "How can you be so *cheerful* in the mornings?" He said, "I feel good, the day is beautiful, and I've got a job."

During summer vacations I worked with him on his jobs, but not by choice. I resented having to spend the seemingly endless days sweeping up after him—the one-man-show of a building contractor—or holding the ladder as he nailed rafters to the ridge, or helping him guide a piece of lumber he was ripping with his power saw. I wanted to be with my friends laying on the beach, or cruising, looking for girls.

But through my frustration I couldn't help but notice how much he enjoyed his work, how he took his time and turned the two-by-four over and over again to see if his cut was precise enough. Every day at four-thirty I would ask him if it was time to go home, and every day he would look up at the waning sky and say, "It's not dark yet," and then laugh.

My father loved working with his sons. He loved teaching us the finer aspects of carpentry: how to read a tape measure; or how to scan a board front and back before you cut it, looking to avoid the insidious knots that could change an easy task into a nightmare. He taught things that seemed so obvious, like when to get down from the ladder and move it, rather than exhaust yourself hanging in some difficult position, trying to nail or cut the awkward eave or rafter. He seemed to be in his glory when we were working with him, and when we were in school, he worked alone. He learned, as a young contractor, that he couldn't keep an employee. He expected the same work ethic that he was brought up with, that we would hear so often from those who lived through the depression years. He hated yelling orders, and even worse, he hated firing men. He learned early in his career that he could do the work of two men, and that having someone there to watch over just slowed him down. Except his boys, who he would tell time and time again that working is a privilege, and how he had started his contracting career when he was eight years old, selling eggs door-to-door in Kansas for the local chicken farmer.

Though I was not with him the day of the accident, it is not hard for me to imagine how amazingly beautiful the morning was at the job site. It's not difficult to picture the low, early sun filtering through the walls of two-by-fours standing in rows like soldiers, their long shadows between the sunlight reflecting off the floating particles of sawdust. Even the huge whine of the saw is heard as music to the carpenter in love with his work, the sweet smell of balsam lingering above the job site for hours after the green lumber is cut. I can see him setting up sawhorses and ladders, laying out the extension cords and lumber he was about to cut. By the age of twelve I had watched him do this a thousand times, or so it seemed back then, when I was still half asleep and trying to fathom the eight hours or more, depending on my father's sense of humor, that I would be prisoner in his world. It seems dream-like now, but then it was the second to the last place I wanted to be—the last, of course, being in church with my mother.

So when I tell you that his sons were in school you'll understand why he was alone the day of the accident, and why he could have been a little distracted by the beautiful morning with its long shadows and sparkling air. The dew had not yet dried on the lumber he was about to cut into thin wood strips, shims to plum and level the door jambs. It is when these rip that many carpenters are led down harm's way, especially those who work alone, who must divide the tasks of aiming the saw blade, guiding the board across the table and lifting the blade guard. It is next to impossible, so, too often the guard is pinned up with a nail or a wooden wedge. And so it was that morning. My father, with his focus on precision, could not have seen that hidden tight knot. Perhaps if his sons were there, a second set of hands would have helped guide the lumber through. Or a second set of eyes would have spotted the hardened pocket before the collision, before the board bucked backward and dragged his fingers into the whirring steel. And, if his sons were there they could have found a salvageable digit to put on ice in his lunch box, and he would not have had to drive himself to the emergency room, his hand wrapped in an old tee shirt held to the headliner.

He came home late that night, his hand, crimson about the fingertips, in a boxing glove of gauze. His face was pale as he crossed the kitchen floor, dreading the news he was about to give his wife. She cried when she saw the dressing, and then got angry as he smiled and tried to tell her it was just a cut.

Hours before sunrise I saw a light on in the living room, and found my father sitting on the sofa, bent over the coffee table, his bandaged hand cradled in his lap. He was writing something on a piece of torn-out notebook paper. "Dad, are you all right?" I asked. He looked up at me with a half-grimace half-smile and told me he was writing a poem, that it helped to take his mind off the pain. I had never known my father to write. Half-asleep I asked him if I could see it, and before I realized what he was doing he had lifted his hand and separated the strips of gauze just enough to show me a strange bloom of swollen red and purple, surrounded by jagged stitches. It made me nauseous, and I could tell it hurt my father to do this for his curious twelve-year-old son. I have never forgotten that heartfelt and painful mis-understanding.

My father is in his seventies now and hasn't needed to

work for years but still puts on his nail bags every day, still drives the upside-down hardware department, still loves his work. On holidays, when the family gets together we talk shop, for as it turned out, I've become a carpenter and contractor myself. Over the years hardly a Christmas goes by that I don't ask him what ever happened to that poem he wrote when he lost his finger, and each time he blushes and laughs and says it's probably in the Smithsonian. I can't help but wonder about that poem, the poem that takes your mind off the pain. Although on those mornings when I'm at the job site, when the light is just so, and the balsam scent sweetens the chilled air, I realize I have become so much like him, a carpenter and contractor. And that I have also learned the poetry of "work with love" from my father, the poet himself, who writes about it rarely, but tries to live it every day.

Bruce Schmidt

A LESSON ON THE SOCCER FIELD

My son Michael was one of the best players on his soccer team and was always very active, aggressive and obviously having fun during every game. However, during this game he looked troubled, maybe sick, and appeared to be going through the motions of playing listlessly, not really into the game. I turned to my wife and asked her if Michael was sick. She said she wasn't aware of him feeling bad.

As the first half ended Michael came off the field nearly crying and soon was crying as a recounting of the on-field events unfolded. The kid that Michael was matched up with on the field had started on him at the very beginning of the game by saying, "We're gonna kick your butt!" Sounds innocent enough but these kids were only seven years old at the time and Michael was very sensitive. He would still climb into bed with us on many nights. Michael's response to the kid was to say, "Shut up!" They had an ongoing exchange that ended with the other kid yelling, "Fuck you!" This bullying, mean behavior had intimidated Michael. When the story was told on the sideline many people got involved and reprimanded the kid. This was an American Youth Soccer Organization (AYSO)-sanctioned game and in AYSO fair play and sportsmanship are encouraged.

Michael sat out the third quarter and I asked him to come away from the sideline crowd so that I could talk to him. He was either embarrassed by his crying or afraid that I was going to be mad at him, and at first he resisted coming to me. Finally he agreed to sit next to a tree and talk with me. I told him that the other player was trying to intimidate him so that he wouldn't play as well. I told him that he would always run into kids who were bullies and would try to intimidate him, and that he had to ignore it and just keep playing as hard and well as he could. I told him that kids who did that usually weren't that good and were trying to make you play worse so they wouldn't lose. I emphasized that he had to stay focused, do his best and forget the asshole.

I was a shy child and when I was intimidated my father would use the then-popular tactic of humiliation, and refer to my behavior as girlish. I threw like a girl, cried like a girl, etc. The father in the movie *The Great Santini* is the extreme example of this method. My father was a very mild version of this but it was all he knew. It never worked well with me. It felt like additional intimidation. What I hoped to do with Michael was to be on his side and support him. That old method seemed like, "Don't be intimidated or I'll intimidate you" or "I'll give you something to cry about." It was fathering by intimidation and threat. The idea was to toughen up the kid and get him ready for a tough world. My goal was the same but the method was to give him understanding and inner strength to keep moving through a sometimes-tough world. To be in his corner with him and not just another face yelling in the crowd.

Michael returned to the game in the fourth quarter with

his team trailing 4-0. He was a new person and looked like the "Tasmanian Devil" cartoon character. He scored two goals and came close to scoring several others. I think this helped him to be stronger in the face of intimidation. He still occasionally gets bullied on and off the playing field, but now he comes right back at any aggressor.

Charlie Bensley

A DAY AT THE BEACH

My two sons, a friend and I went to the beach for a week-day afternoon. There were no lifeguards on duty and no one else nearby. I sat in a chair and read while the three boys played on the beach and in the surf, throwing a ball back and forth. After we had been there awhile I remembered that I had to call work and the only phone available was near the road behind the beach. Most importantly the phone was well out of sight of the beach.

My older son Eric is a very strong-willed, sometimes defiant boy. He learns by doing. For example, if he is warned not to do something because it would be bad for him, he has to do it himself and get hurt. In jest I say that I hope he doesn't try something like stepping in front of a moving bus but he might. He is that stubborn and independent.

I decided to leave them on the beach while I went to make the call. But before I did I told them where I was going, that I wouldn't be gone very long and that they should not go in the water. I emphasized the part about them not going in the water. I asked them, in particular Eric, to repeat back to me what I had said. They all acknowledged that they were not to go into the water and that they would not.

I made my call and returned to the beach within fifteen minutes. As the beach came into view I first noticed Eric lying on the sand breathing hard. I was shocked and asked what had happened, already knowing everything but the exact details. Eric had waded into the water to get the ball, and the ball was drifting increasingly farther away from the beach. Eric had traveled far enough out that the undertow pulled him out farther still and he had to swim hard to get back in. He said that at one point he thought that he wouldn't make it. He was still gasping for air as he finished his story. I'm not sure what I said or did. I was very upset and asked several times if my instructions had been clear. Everyone assured me that they had been. The explanation had to do with the ball getting farther out and Eric not being aware of the undertow. Eric was very contrite in his responses—unusual for him—and an indication of how shook up he was.

I thought about what to do about his behavior. In particular I was asking myself what punishment I thought was appropriate. The more I thought about it, the more I thought a traditional punishment like a grounding, major room time, a refusal to let him attend an exciting event or a work project would be counterproductive. Often the punishment and the justice or injustice of that punishment can become the focus while the infraction itself falls into the background. I didn't want that to happen in this case. I wanted Eric to learn from this. I told him he had to write me a story about the incident, what it meant to him, and what, if anything, he had learned.

He wrote about how scared he had been when he wasn't

sure he would be able to swim back. He also wrote, "Dad knows what's best for me sometimes and I don't, and I need to listen to him." A major breakthrough for Eric! I keep that story handy for future use.

Charlie Bensley

.

DADDY: MY BEST FRIEND

My father was a strong, vibrant, intelligent, serious and distinguished-looking gentleman. He was loved by many and disliked by many. He seemed to be going somewhere all the time, running here and there in his Kangol hat with a jug of water, riding high in his truck. Throughout the years, he owned several big trucks, usually Ford F150s or F250s. These trucks seemed to fit his personality and just naturally seemed to be a part of him. He "really used" the trucks that he owned at the time. On the seat and floor were strewn spoons, forks, glasses, mail, toothbrushes, deodorant, etc., which gave it a "lived-in" effect. He hauled items as small as nails and as big as doors, windows, carpet and lumber.

His moods fluctuated daily. Some days he laughed heartily and enjoyed jokes and visits from friends, other days he preferred quiet and solitude. One had to be perceptive to recognize these moods and understand when to visit or not, when to come and when to go, and when to talk and when to be quiet. In his "up" moods, he'd talk for hours about his childhood or some experience he had. He'd recall times he'd bought tickets from scalpers for the World Series games, and then laugh at the memory of a friend who pretended to be physically handicapped so he'd be afforded a good view of the game in a section for wheelchairs. He also talked for hours about people who tried to take advantage of him and of how we must count our money in the bank because bank tellers make mistakes legally and illegally. But he was soft-spoken as he recalled a lost love—my mother—whom he mistreated at times. His voice and eyes reflected the agony and sadness of not being able to go back to yesterday to make amends to her and to "do it all over again—and do it right by her."

My father's wisdom was reflected in his interactions with people. He often displayed great insight as he described people and their tendencies. Dad saw right through people who tried to swindle and those who were superficial. He kept a watchful eye on those who were sneaky. He didn't give the time of day to those who were greedy, but he'd bend over backward to help those who were real. My father's wisdom showed through his vision for he always planned ahead. He planned everything in his head and moved strategically to execute his plan in a timely manner. My dad followed through even when others told him to rest or that he couldn't do it, because he had contemplated the idea for quite some time. He never allowed others to influence his plan because he was sure of himself and what he wanted to do. From time to time, he would ask my opinion of his plans. I approved whatever he wanted to do, after he carefully gave me the road map of how and why. I usually blessed his plan and advised him to do whatever made him happy and satisfied. These blessings not only included his plans for career advancement, but also for his personal relationships.

I witnessed the side of him that yelled and disagreed with people—their ideas, ways and actions. I also witnessed his meekness, humbleness and sensitivity to others as he empathized with their plights—then gave repeatedly to them. It was natural for him to send money to the sick or to share food (fruit, vegetables, etc.) when he bought them in bulk.

He lacked empathy for people who were healthy and did not work. He believed in hard work. As a child, he never permitted me or my sisters and brothers to sleep or lie in bed during the day. We had to be busy. We ironed everything that could be ironed—sheets, pillowcases, underclothes—you name it. We waxed and buffed the hardwood floors with our hands and feet. We washed the mirrors and shined the furniture because he felt that idleness was the devil's workshop. He served as an example by working two jobs and sometimes three. Even when life's valleys and a devastating illness consumed him, he continued to plan and to work. He continued to count and figure in his head. He continued to deal and interact and give consultation to people seeking help.

My father influenced my life in many ways, but one incident in particular stands out. When I was seven years old, my father was severely burned from his head to his toes. He was thrown out of his truck when tanks, which he was transporting on the back of it, exploded. His burns were less severe than they might have been because he rolled into a nearby ditch containing water. When my siblings and I were able to visit him in the hospital, he was scary. Pink flesh was visible where dark skin used to be. We were afraid to go near him and stood huddled together at the door. Over the weeks and months that followed I witnessed my father withstand the pain as his skin healed. He returned to work, before healing completely, all pink and scarred. His ability to withstand pain without complaining and to return to work while still in pain marked my life in that I felt I could endure life's difficulties and keep going. I learned to alter the way I viewed and dealt with difficulties when I could not change them. Because of him I am able to weather storms, accept challenges and make the best of everything that life sends my way.

I'd like to remember my friend, my daddy, as a tall, strong, confident, broad-shouldered man, but flashes of days during his illness shine like bright beacons before me. I watched him trying to hold on to his strength and his pride by attempting to walk when he couldn't, trying to take a shower when he couldn't, trying to smile when he couldn't and trying to eat when he couldn't eat. He seized every opportunity to teach me something—some lesson about life or some lesson about the business. My own selfish direction was focused toward making his home immaculate during his illness, but he would often tell me to put the mop down and just talk to him. I sat for a while, but up I jumped since my mind was on cleaning. Of course, there were many, many times at night when the house was quiet that we had long conversations—conversations that have been imprinted in my memory.

The last morning of his life is etched in my heart. He ate salmon and a biscuit (one of his favorite meals) and sat quietly upright in bed. He watched everyone who passed his bed. There was a serene look about him as he was happy that he was not alone. I was there with him and for him as he was for me throughout my life. I will always love and never forget my best friend, my hero, my mentor—my daddy.

Shelley Wyckoff

THE CRUSH

I will never hear a train whistle without thinking about my father, Maurice Steenburgen. His father and grandfather were railroad men, and he followed suit as a freight-train conductor for the Missouri Pacific Railroad. He worked on the rails his whole life to provide for our family of four. He bought a little house in North Little Rock, Arkansas, and spent his life paying it off a little at a time. My sister and I were raised there and my mother still lives there. The house is resonant with love and memories of when I was called Mary Nell, and when I say I'm going home—that's where I mean.

My dad was a man of very few words, and the best listener I've ever known. He didn't attend college but he was just plain wise. Like many wise people, he was filled with wonder. I remember walking into a room in an old house that I had rented in Sneden's Landing, New York. My dad was there, staring up at a low beam of the ceiling.

"What are you looking at?" I asked him.

"Mary," he asked, "how *old* is this house?"

Daddy took in life with an extraordinary appreciation for it and wondered about everything as if the whole world were held together by magic. I never heard him complain (he called it bellyachin') about anything. He never protested about how hard he worked, climbing all over those trains, all hours of the night; never about the seven heart attacks he suffered that could not make his beautiful heart stop beating; and never even about the cancer that finally killed him. I think that he felt the privilege of life itself. He was, in his quiet way, as heroic a soul as I will ever know.

My father would get his call to come to work at all hours of the night and morning. He would pack his black "grip" and be gone for a couple of days, the end of the line being Poplar Bluff, Missouri. We only had one car and I was too little to be left alone, so my mom and I would take him to work in the old Chevy. I would practically do this in my sleep. I would rouse up enough to say bye to him while peeking through sleepy eyes at that Arkansas train yard at 3 A.M., 4 A.M., and often in the rosy dawn light. Then I'd sleep all the way home. Twenty-five years later I returned there and produced a movie called *End of the Line*. It was about our life—the railroad life—and no film was ever created with more respect and love.

To my father, I was pretty much the greatest actor of all time. When I was a young actress, and in reality a waitress in New York City, my father called me "Soop." Soop was short for superstar and it didn't matter a bit to him that I was a waitress for six years. The fact that I was *trying* to do something as magical as being an actor was good enough for him. He memorized the brochure from my school, the Neighborhood Playhouse, and was very fond of tossing little tidbits of information into conversations with his gin-rummy buddies like, "Are you aware that Bobby Duvall and Gregory Peck *both* studied at the Neighborhood

Playhouse?" I think most people thought that he was crazy to be so happy about his daughter going off to big, scary New York. He just responded to my heart's ferocious desire with a belief that I would do just fine. In 1977, when I called him from Jack Nicholson's Paramount Studios office to say that I had just been cast opposite Nicholson as the leading lady of *Goin' South*, he didn't sound a bit surprised. His belief in me was that simple—that real.

My father died in 1989, during the filming of *Parenthood*. I had traveled back and forth to Arkansas to be with him during the last months. I had just arrived back in Orlando to continue filming when I got the call to turn around and come home. When I was changing planes in Atlanta I called my sister and found out that I wouldn't make it in time. He was already gone. I stumbled, alone, into a stall in the ladies room and stood there, crying silently in grief. However, I knew at that moment that to blame myself forever for not being there at the instant of his death would be to eclipse an amazing relationship. I knew that I was as loved as a daughter could be, and he knew that he was cherished as a father and that I could not have asked for more. We each thought that the other had hung the moon.

I probably should stop my story here. The other thing I want to tell will probably make most people think I'm crazy. But it's my truth about my father and I would feel remiss in writing about him without including it.

The day after Daddy died, our tiny house filled with people. They were nurturing and comforting, as folks from my part of the country tend to be, but I still felt lonely. My

mother and my sister were close to people there and I was
feeling the distance of my many years of living far away. I
was also going through a divorce, and it was a hard time for
me to "lose" the other man in my life. My dad had known
that I was very confused and that I had a deep desire to look
at my part in my failed marriage so that I might not make
the same mistakes in my future relationships. I had been
married to a wonderful person, but I felt that I had lost my
way somehow. (Ten years later, I look back and feel very
differently. I'm grateful for every step of this journey, even
the seemingly faltering steps.)

The other thing you must know has to do with my heart's
first crush. When I was in first grade I fell in love with a
boy named Tommy Hill. It was fairly unrequited. Actually,
it was *painfully* unrequited. I wrote him a note that looked
like this:

> Do you love me?
> Check YES   ☐
> Check NO   ☐

He checked: NO   ☑

I told my father about my crush and he began the gentle
teasing that continued throughout my school years. Long
after Tommy and I were old enough to actually date, but
didn't, Daddy still held on. "Tommy Hill . . . Tommy Hill"
he would sing the name in his slow, soft drawl. Tommy and
I went to different high schools. I dated Randy Barker, but
still Daddy would chant and make me laugh with his,
"Tommy Hill . . . Tommy Hill."

So the day after he died, I sat in my father's chair,

surrounded by people, missing him, wondering what was wrong with me and relationships and aching with loneliness. Suddenly, I felt a strange feeling. The air seemed to get thick and sound began to be muted. Something was about to happen. I looked up and out the window and there, walking up the drive to our front porch, was Tommy Hill. I went to the door and smiled into his beautiful, bespectacled, grown-up face. As I let him in he said, "Mary Nell, I hope you don't mind my coming. I can't really say why I'm here. But all morning long something's just made me come." I said, "Well, I have a pretty good idea *who* made you come. Sit down."

I know it sounds crazy but Daddy did all that. He made Tommy get up and put on a beautiful blue suit and risk embarrassment to go see an old friend from many years ago. Tommy comforted me that day. He made me laugh. He said everything just right to someone who was hurting hard. He gave of himself and I understood. My father wasn't playing matchmaker. Tommy was happily in love with a beautiful woman I had known in college. Daddy simply wanted me to revisit the first object of my heart's desire. All I had to do was go back to Mary Nell. To the little girl who had spotted a class act at six years old—and then I would be just fine.

You could argue all kinds of ways that my dad didn't orchestrate it all that day. But I'll never, ever be convinced otherwise. I felt his hand in it and, anyway, it's just how he would have done it. And today I smile at the man whom I have been in a joyous relationship with for five-and-one-half years and I bless Daddy for helping me find my way to him. For our wedding present, my mother gave Ted and me the only possession I have of my father's. It is a small, steel lantern that he used to signal the engineers and brakemen on the railroad. It was a perfect gift. Even after his death, he has continued to illuminate my journey.

I hear a train whistle in the night and I know he's out there. And why should I doubt that Daddy would move Heaven and Earth to help me find my way? After all, it was he who hung the moon.

Mary Steenburgen

OKAY, OLD MAN, NOW AT LAST WE'RE PEERS!

Almost twenty years have passed since my father died. Thinking back on my relationship with him, I see it in various phases: My first fifteen years at home, the next ten years, then the ten years or so after that until Father died and now the last twenty years. This is also my life span, and I mention the whole of it, because my father has been important to me in many different ways throughout it all. There is no one single incident that has affected me so deeply that it stands out clearly as *the* experience for me.

Maybe this is symptomatic of many men's relationships to their fathers: If he is present, he is usually in the background and his contributions are not very conspicuous. Not very many are as inaccessible and solitary as the father in Paul Auster's book, *The Invention of Solitude*, but very few fathers have been as present and active and caring as we all could have wished.

My first fifteen years was in a family of five children. I was the second oldest and the first son. Mother, an educated nurse, was a full-time housewife. Even in the 1950s, we had a maid, helping us with the domestic chores. Father was a theologian. He was not ordained a minister until he was

sixty-five. He had served his last five years as head pastor
of several parishes, but most of his life he was director of a
church institute of education, which required of him a mix-
ture of vision, research knowledge, management, lobbying
and entrepreneurial spirit. He put a lot of energy into his
work. First I had thought of writing that he "enjoyed" this
life, but that word did not quite fit. My father was something of an ascetic puritan, and his life was solidly based on
a strong sense of calling and duty. As a boy, I thought that
if he had not met my mother, he would have loved to be a
monk. He was respected. I think I sensed that dimension
when I saw him with his staff and friends: he was highly
respected—almost revered. That gave me a feeling of pride,
but also a certain distance.

Mother has told me that father took a lot of pride in us
when we were children. I cannot imagine that he partici-
pated very much in our daily care. But I can remember him
washing dishes, which he actually did regularly, and he also
helped us organize our domestic duties. I enjoyed being
allowed to prepare food, but detested washing dishes. And
then there was the garden work. I guess he must have disliked it himself, because he always spoke of our duty and
obligation when he asked us to do the gardening chores.

From my earliest years I have a much clearer memory of
my grandfather, who, when visiting, always wanted to take
me away from town and back to his farm. I really enjoyed
that. He also took me with him on all his travels throughout
the area. He allowed me to help in the cow barn—especially
with the horses, which was what I loved the most.

But two contributions from Father appear clearly when I

reminisce about my first fifteen years. First, I recall the stories. I really cherished the long Sunday mornings in my
parents' bed, when Father told stories, especially the heroic
one about when he scared away a burglar who tried to get
into the house, and how he chased him down the street. He
also told several stories about the war. The Germans had
imprisoned my grandfather during the last two years of the
war, and my parents had moved up to my grandmother's
house after I was born in 1943. Father was active in the
local resistance movement, and stories from that time made
a special impact on me because I had grown up in Norway
following the war.

I had a particular liking for stories from his own childhood on the Norwegian West Coast, especially the one about
when his father, after a season of fishing outside Iceland,
had brought home on a boat a little, capricious Icelandic
horse. The horse was grazing in their pasture, and my father,
then six, was asked to go and get it. He brought a halter and
went to the huge pasture. When he got close to the horse, it
ran away. That happened several times—and when telling
about it, my father really knew how to make that incident
dramatic. Finally he had become so despondent and desper-
ate that he just sat down on a rock, crying with his head in
his hands. Suddenly he felt a soft, wet muzzle on his cheek,
and there was the Icelandic horse just waiting to be har-
nessed and taken to the barn. These stories always had some
good moral, but surprisingly enough I cannot remember that
Father overdid that part of it.

The other contribution was when Father took time to play
with us. It was not often. His own childhood had been

partly ruined by an illness that had lasted for several years and had kept him away from playgrounds, school and sports. Instead he had become an avid reader.

When I was a boy, he rarely had time to play with us during the school year, but during holiday seasons he allowed himself to play a little more. He once walked with us from our cabin in the mountains up to a little stream. He brought a spade and helped us build a little dam to form a pond where we could swim. Then we constructed a waterwheel and made a play-sized sawmill, and floated logs down the brook. That was great! But the one incident from our vacations in the mountains that I remember the most was once when all the kids and adults played hide-and-seek together. I was probably around ten. It must have been on Father's birthday in July, because we were several families together. This hide-and-seek game was a special variant where those who had been found ("the prisoners") could be freed again. It required a lot of moving around while hiding, and in between giving signs to free the prisoners. I still love to play that with kids. At that time it probably gave us kids a sense of both community and equality, because the adults were not much better at it than we were.

Father did not take much part in our sports. In spite of the illness of his childhood and the snow-less winters out West, he was still a fairly good skier, and a few times he took me along for cross-country treks. I can remember one trek when I was about eleven that I came to understand that I had become a better skier than he was. That was probably the first time I really acknowledged that father had become old. After that, when I got into my teens, my father, of course, became increasingly obsolete to me.

All of which brings me into the next ten years, when I began to move away from home. Since we lived in Oslo, it actually saved me a lot of money to be allowed to keep my room back home while studying at the university. And except for one year studying in the U.S. and half a year at the university in Trondheim, I lived at home until I was twenty-five.

I don't think that was a smart thing to do. It took me a long time to dare a cautious revolt and acquire some independence. My oldest sister had left home (smart woman) while I remained as the first of my siblings to break some new ground with my very conservative parents as to dating and bringing my girlfriend home. I must have been almost twenty when I first dared to protest against the domestic rules. My parents were still able to exert an unbelievable amount of control—Mother with her more dramatic, irrational modes; Father with his distant, mild manners. When he talked with me about our disagreements, he almost always pushed Mother in front of him. He would tell me that she had been awake all night because of this and that she had become so depressed. Unconsciously I think I inherited some of Father's conflict avoidance and mild dominance. It has taken me quite some time to find out about these things.

But he also gave me a positive introduction into the world of work, and now I speak of academic work, which I definitely sensed that he loved, in contrast to the gardening. I was allowed to visit him in Germany when he was on a study leave. I was almost sixteen and had learned a little

German. (He made his doctoral dissertation when he was
more than fifty years old.) I remember one winter vacation
week, my last year in senior high school. The rest of the
family was away, and Father and I went to the university
library early every morning, and sat there studying and
reading all day, Father for his dissertation and I for my final
exams. I felt like a genuine scholar. That really was an initiation into academia!

Marrying my girlfriend when almost twenty-five was a
good breakaway from home. This was the period when
father was most distant from me. My wife and I lived far
north most of the time. My political views had become
quite different from those of my parents, and the lifestyle of
our new family was ages away from what I experienced as
the old folks' bourgeois mode of living. When we had our
daughter I could, however, see how delighted he was, how
good he was at creating a bond with her and how he enjoyed
playing with her.

One incident stands out from this period. Mother had
been seriously injured in a car accident, and spent four
months in the hospital. That made Father really old. I
remember coming south to visit Mother after I had heard
about it. Father picked me up at the railway station. He was
simply crushed, and was disclosing and expressing feelings
in a way that I had never experienced with him before.
Going home with him afterwards also revealed how help-
less he was alone without Mother. The strong, much revered
professional was totally dependent on Mother, both emotionally and practically.

A year after Mother's accident, I came south again after

a breakup in my marriage. I did not experience much support from my parents then. They were not able to talk much about my situation. Most of their concern was not about how it was for me, or if I needed any support, but about more superficial or formal details. A couple of years after Mother's accident, my father was diagnosed with cancer. As his condition worsened, it was depressing for me (as well as for my mother) to see how little Father was able to feel or be realistic about what was happening to himself with death approaching. He died a year-and-a-half later.

I had been seeing a psychologist for a while before his death—first of all because I needed to understand more about the mess the divorce had represented for me, but also because it gave me a good opportunity to reevaluate what in my life was my own stuff and what was my father's. This period also set off the last phase of twenty years in my relationship to my father.

This has been a period of anger and reconciliation, grief and gratitude. It took some time to be more familiar with the loss and bereavement, and it took even more time (and courage!) to approach my anger connected to it. The feeling of grief after his death came gradually when I allowed myself to feel some bitterness about what he had not been able to give to me. He had been so distant. Eventually it developed into longing. And with help from a good friend I was able to see more of what he had meant to me, all the good incidents I had experienced and all the qualities he had represented. This led into a process very much like atonement.

This process has been a necessary part of my own

growth as man and father. Today I think I can look back on my father with a settled sense of gratitude and also with a conciliatory clarity about our differences and disagreements. Once in a while I go for a meeting at his former institute. In the boardroom where we usually gather, there is a painted portrait of my father on the wall. The painting has that mild, distant expression that often characterized him. Once in a while he looks down on me, and I can see he has let me go now. And I look back up on him again, with a little bit of that old pride I used to have, but also with the grown-up son's egalitarian understanding: Okay, old man, now at last we're peers!

Berger J. Hareide

MY FATHER, PA

I am one of ten children of a coal miner and a domestic worker. Each parent was strong, but my father's strength was of a quiet nature. My father taught me how to make a point and maintain inner peace—walk joyful but carry a big stick. He also taught me to smile and have humor, even in the most dismal situation. He taught me how to love unconditionally.

There were three sons in my family, but no outsiders other than older relatives knew that two of the three sons were really my father's stepsons. Why? Because they were totally accepted as my father's sons. In fact, one of my brother's sons became aware of this fact only at the death of my father in 1994. This grandson physically looked like and had the mannerisms of my father. In fact, my father's first airplane trip was to attend this grandson's wedding out West. My father never faltered in his love and acceptance of each of us. He always played, laughed, loved and disciplined as if we were all his natural own. Playmates would always say, "Your dad is so nice. He loves all of us." Our house was always full of other children and our dad always was proud of the "flock."

My daddy. I called him Pa, always had a smile on his face. When he walked into a room, it lit up. He didn't have to speak a word. Even when he'd come to school because of trouble we had gotten into, he had a smile, though he was dead serious. Adults had a problem reading his smile, but we learned well how to use this skill. Some people have poker faces. My dad had a "smiley face." Through his actions, he taught us to support what was right. I remember being told about a time when my older brother was at home on leave from the military. This happened in the late fifties or early sixties. A cashier in the state-owned liquor store was trying to cheat him out of his change. My father was summoned to the store by one of his friends because the incident was escalating toward violence. My father, who always wore Liberty overalls, went to the store, walked in, spoke to my brother, turned to the cashier and said, "Give my boy his money." The cashier obeyed. Dad said, "Let's go, son," and they left the store. Reports have it that my father never lost his smile and never took his hands from the pockets of his overalls. My father commanded respect, giving it freely to those deemed worthy of it. He taught us that respect is something earned, not just given. My father's actions were truly done in the spirit of love, for it took place in the segregated, volatile South.

My dad taught us to have humor and laugh, to not take ourselves so seriously. He used his humor and laughter to solve problems. For example, when the coal miners would go on strike or there were layoffs, he, though worried, never appeared unsettled. Instead, he would locate alternative work to support the family. He helped all of us to see that hard, honest work was not beneath us. All of the children developed a willingness to work as young adults, and that attitude has provided each of us with solid professions and careers.

Even to his death, my father was everybody's daddy. All the little children in my neighborhood called him Granddaddy. His caring eyes monitored and guarded them each day as they departed the school bus and headed home at the close of the school day, safe and protected by my daddy, Pa.

JoAnne McLinn

Contributors

Gabriel Arquilevich, a father and stepfather, is a writer living in Ojai, California. He is a teacher and tutor of young writers.

Charlie Bensley is the father of two boys and a businessman in Los Angeles, where he also coaches youth sports.

Connie Nicholas Carnes is Clinical Director of the National Children's Advocacy Center. She is a wife and mother, and a nationally known expert in the field of child-abuse evaluation and treatment.

Berger Hareide is the father of a college-age daughter and a stepfather. He is codirector of the internationally renowned Marriage and Family Study Center in Norway. He is a respected educator, author and ethicist, and active in his church on a local and national level.

Melbourne Henry grew up in Jamaica. He is the father of two daughters and formerly a distinguished college professor and administrator. He is director of health services for the Alaska Department of Corrections.

James B. Hill, a decorated pilot during World War II, is a retired jeweler. He is an active father and grandfather, a historian and Sunday school teacher.

JoAnne McLinn is a devoted aunt and director of field practicum education at the graduate social work program at Alabama A&M University.

Bruce L. Schmidt is the father of two children, a builder and a contractor. He is a poet and songwriter.

Earnest L. Starks, LTC Ret., following a distinguished career in the United States Army is now a graduate student at Alabama A&M University. He is a devoted single father and a university tennis coach and is active in working with youth in his community.

Mary Steenburgen is the loving mother of two children and the daughter of a railroad man. She is an Academy Award-winning actress and widely known for her humanitarian activities.

Shelley Ann Wyckoff is the mother of two college-age daughters and director of the department of social work at Alabama A&M University.

Bibliography

Armour, Stephanie. "Dad Is Job One: Paternity Leaves Increasingly Popular." *USA Today*, 23 February 1998, sec. B, p. 1.

Bly, Robert, James Hillman and Michael Meade, eds. *The Rag and Bone Shop of the Heart: A Poetry Anthology*. New York: HarperCollins Publishers, 1992.

Bronfenbrenner, U. "Discovering What Families Do." In *Rebuilding the Nest: A New Commitment to the American Family*. Milwaukee, Wis.: Family Service American, 1990.

Brown, Raymond E. *An Introduction to the New Testament*. New York: Doubleday Publishing, 1997.

Cobern, Camden M. *The New Archeological Discoveries: And Their Bearing Upon the New Testament*. New York: Funk and Wagnalls, 1917.

Coles, Robert. *The Moral Intelligence of Children*. New York: Random House, 1997.

Douglas-Klotz, Neil. *Desert Wisdom: Sacred Middle Eastern Writings from the Goddess Through the Sufis*. New York: HarperCollins Publishers, 1995.

Ellis, E. J. *The Poetical Works of William Blake*. London: Chatoo and Windus, 1906.

Faulkner, R. *The Egyptian Book of the Dead*. San Francisco: Chronicle Books, 1994.

Gandhi, Virchend R. *The Unknown Life of Jesus Christ*. Chicago: Progressive Thinker Publishing House, 1907.

187

Gardner, Howard. *Frames of Mind.* New York: Basic Books Inc., 1983.

Gibran, Kahlil. *Jesus.* New York: Alfred A. Knopf, 1928.

Ginsburg, C. D. *The Essenes: Their History and Doctrine and The Kabbalah: Its Doctrines, Development and Literature.* New York: The MacMillan Company, 1956.

Goleman, Daniel. *Emotional Intelligence.* New York: Bantam Books, 1995.

Hartmann, F. *The Life of Jehoshua.* London: Occult Publishing Co., 1889.

Hodson, G. *The Christ Life from Nativity to Ascension.* Wheaton, Ill.: The Theosophical Publishing House, 1975.

Hoeller, Stephan A. *Jung and the Lost Gospels.* Wheaton, Ill.: Quest Books, 1989.

Hooven, Carole, John Mordechai Gottman, and Lynn Fainsilber Katz. "Parental Meta-Emotion Structure Predicts Family and Child Outcomes." *Cognition and Emotion* 9.2/3 (1995): 229–264.

Massey, Gerald. *Ancient Egypt: The Light of the World.* London: Richard Clay & Sons Ltd., 1907.

Mead, G. R. S. *Did Jesus Live 100 B.C.?* London: Theosophical Publishing Society, 1903.

Miller, Calvin, ed. *The Book of Jesus.* New York: Simon & Schuster, 1996.

Mitchell, Stephen. *The Gospel According to Jesus.* New York: Harper Perennial, 1993.

Moore, Thomas. *Care of the Soul.* New York: HarperCollins Publishers, 1992.

The New Jerusalem Bible. New York: Doubleday, 1990.

Notovitch, N. *The Unknown Life of Jesus Christ.* New York: Rand, McNally & Co., 1894.

Osborn, Diane K., ed. *A Joseph Campbell Companion: Reflections on the Art of Living.* New York: HarperCollins Publishers, 1991.

Partington, Angela, ed. *The Oxford Dictionary of Quotations.* New York: Oxford University Press, 1992.

Popenoe, David. "A World Without Fathers." *Wilson Quarterly* 20.2 (Spring 1996):12.

——. *Life Without Father: Compelling New Evidence That Fatherhood and Marriage Are Indispensable for the Good of Children and Society.* New York: Free Press, 1997.

Sanders, E. P., and Margaret Davies. *Studying the Synoptic Gospels.* Valley Forge, Pa: Trinity Press International, 1989.

Steiner, Rudolf. *Christianity as Mystical Fact.* London: Rudolf Steiner Press, 1914.

Teilhard de Chardin, Pierre. *The Divine Milieu.* New York: Harper & Bros., 1960.

About the Author

John L. Hart, Ph.D., is a father and a stepfather. He is presently an associate professor at the School of Social Work, New Mexico Highlands University. Dr. Hart is well known among corporate, professional and Christian groups as an inspirational and motivational speaker. He has been a consultant to the Norwegian National Fathering Project and the Samlivssenteret (Family Life Center) of Norway for several years. Dr. Hart is also a poet and a Vietnam veteran. He lives with his wife in Montezuma, New Mexico.

Becoming a Father is the first book in Dr. Hart's Joseph trilogy. He is currently writing the second and third books in this fathering trilogy. The second book is about fathering teens and young adults, while the third book is about the experience of being the father of a child who dies or is severely disabled. To submit an inspirational story that you feel would be appropriate for one of these upcoming books, or to contact Dr. Hart about speaking to your organization, write or call him at:

Dr. John L. Hart
NMHU Box 9154
Las Vegas, NM 87701
(505) 454-3563
fax: (505) 454-3290
email: *johnhart@merlin.nmhu.edu*